Oh Grandma, You're Kidding

Memories of 75 Years in the Great Plains

Gladys S. Douglass

J & L Lee Co.
Lincoln, Nebraska

All photos are from the collections of the author and publisher with the exception of those on pages 13, 44, 60, 71, 79, 88 and 99 which are from the photo collection of the Nebraska State Historical Society.

Portions of this book have appeared in variously edited forms in the Lincoln *Sunday Journal and Star*, grateful acknowledgment is made for their permission to reprint.

ISBN 0-934904-00-6

TABLE OF CONTENTS

PREFACE

This book really began when I was a little girl, listening to my mother tell us stories of her own childhood. She was born in the U.S. Centennial year of 1876 on a farm four miles southeast of Woodbine, Iowa, which is near Missouri Valley and not far from Omaha.

Mother was an excellent storyteller; she put in the little details which bring the past vividly to life. Small children always loved her; she never talked down to them. She would play their games with them as if she were the same age, and she always played to win.

We children who listened were Gladys, born March 1, 1901; Adrian, born November 29, 1902; and Irene, born November 20, 1904. Marjorie, the youngest sister, came along so much later that she doesn't remember Mother's early story-telling at all.

When my own children were old enough, their grandmother told them the same tales and I listened again. The stories grew a little with the years (I know now that one remembers more of childhood as one grows older).

Soon Mother began to tell my children stories of my own early years. Sometimes I wonder if I remember some of these happenings or if I remember hearing Mother tell them thirty years after they happened. Certainly this has reinforced my memory.

I, too, told the same stories to my children and again to my grand-children when I was lucky enough to have them with me. As the little ones grew older, they found it hard to believe that my world had ever been so different from theirs. "Oh Grandma, you're kidding," they would chorus.

Years later, when my eldest granddaughter, Kelly, was writing a UCLA senior's term paper about the early twentieth century, she asked me to write down some of my memories for her. That was in 1979 and I wrote quite a lot. She got an A + on her paper.

In 1981, I showed the long manuscript to the editor of Focus Magazine in the office of Lincoln's Sunday Journal and Star and he asked me to write short pieces about many of the incidents I had mentioned. They have been appearing in the newspaper from time to time ever since.

I could never have finished these stories for publication without the help of very many people. I did research at the Nebraska State Historical Society where the staff helped me find what I needed and were very pleased about it.

During the nearly two years I have spent writing the short pieces, I bothered many friends of my generation. I tried to write down only the truth about those early years of the century, but I did not trust memory; I asked these friends.

It was impossible to check purely family memories — my brother and next sister are gone, and my younger sister does not remember much of these early years. The Reference Department of the Bennett Martin Public Library was another big help. The staff helped me find books I needed — about vaudeville, for instance.

Most of all, I owe grateful thanks to my friend and editor, Dale Griffing. Until his retirement early in 1983, he edited all the pieces which went into Focus and he suggested that I write short articles about incidents which I mentioned in the very long manuscript which he read in 1981.

He was always pleasant and patient — making only minimal, corrective changes in my copy because, as he said, he wanted them to reflect my memories and time, not his. After retirement he edited the later pieces which I wrote with this book in view.

Sigrid Tehrani, who now edits Focus, has also been pleasant to work with and lets me write my own way, that of a *storyteller*, not of a writer of literature.

I hope the friends who are a year or two younger than I will forgive me when I name them as being "about my age."

And I fervently hope that I have not left any out.

Perhaps Marie Becker and Meda Knapp helped the most. They lived in my childhood neighborhood — one block down the street — and both have remarkable memories. They never showed the least impatience to me as I badgered them continually during the early writings. And very often, each would expand her answer into a reminiscence which triggered my memory into something different.

There are still living in Lincoln two of my Elliott School eighth grade classmates (we graduated in 1915). They helped with my memories of Elliott, Lincoln High School and our University of Nebraska years. We had many pleasant meetings and I bothered each of them often on the phone. They lent me pictures (All of mine were lost in a fire in 1924 in my mother's attic. The few I have now were hanging in her bedroom). These two old friends are Belle Farman and Edith Hornby and I hope they have enjoyed remembering as much as I have.

ii

Other old friends from high school years have given me unending help and encouragement. They include Grace Marks, Mary Guthrie, Steve Gilbert, Evar Anderson, Harold Clute, Flavia Champe and John Lawlor. Steve was particularly helpful with his memories of a village childhood.

My last visits with the late Jeannette Farquhar and Clarice Hicks added valuable facts to the store of material that I drew upon.

I even bothered people in their nineties. John Selleck was very helpful with the football article and Aileen Cochrane and Mabel Lee gave me helpful suggestions.

Dr. Paul Bancroft, who was a stranger until we "met" on the telephone, told me interesting stories about his doctor grandfather.

I received very many letters when my articles began to appear in Focus Magazine. Quite a few were from people whom I taught during the twenties (I taught school for five years before my marriage). I enjoyed their letters very much and I have agreed to go to one high school class reunion in 1986. I hope to live that long.

Special thanks go to former student Dr. Howard Mitchell, who read my medical piece, and to Theodore Damme, who lives in Denver. His brother in Talmage had sent him some of my pieces. Ted sent a generous check to help with postage and has written me often.

I heard from old friends, acquaintances and complete strangers. I thank the Sunday Journal and Star for forwarding some of the mail.

To you nice people: I am sorry that I haven't answered all of your letters. I was so busy living my non-writing life—gardening, knitting a big afghan against time to enter in a contest, etc.—that I got too far behind. I have all of your letters and still hope to answer them.

Then I must thank younger friends who did not share my very ancient memories but who told me stories they had heard as children. They also saved tearsheets of my articles to send to friends and relatives from away.

Special thanks for visits and encouragement go to Mary Beechner, Sheila Graf, my young neighbor Susan Renken, and to Earl and Barbara Barnawell, who have read my articles, fed me and treated me like a grandmother.

I also thank those who gathered tearsheets from their neighbors (often five or more copies of each article). These were Louise Isgrig, Florence Mitchel and Dorothea Heckman. Several other friends sent me one copy of each piece.

This list cannot go on forever, so I will close with thanks for my publisher, Jim McKee. Jim is an authority on old Lincoln and I often called him for help, long before I knew he was to be my publisher.

There is a special mother's thanks for my daughter, Ann Kelley, who did my washing and my shopping while I wrote, and who read and criticized my rough drafts without mercy or bias. She also reminded me if I left out one of her favorite stories.

Last I want to thank Emily Griffing who did the final typing on the last ten pieces I wrote and to my granddaughter, Carey Kelley, who typed most of the rest in their final form.

Gladys Douglass
September, 1983

DEDICATION

To my mother Anna McDunn Schaaf who showed me how to tell stories and to my eldest granddaughter Kelly Anne Douglass who talked me into writing them down.

iv

NEBRASKA AND LINCOLN
IN THE EARLY DAYS

When I told these stories to my grandchildren, they would say, "Oh Grandma! You're kidding!" They could not believe in my childhood world without TV, air conditioning, the "fridge", self-starting automobiles and most electric appliances. In my world before the first World War, all these, and very many other modern comforts and extravagances, were missing. However, we had clean air, a great deal less noise around us, and the stars showed clearly as they will never appear to us again. The World War sparked the change that would affect our lives, our homes, cities and our manners and morals. An adult Lincoln citizen of 1907 or 1910 would not have believed in our world of today. I have lived to see it all change and sometimes I'm not sure it is real.

So here you are, kids—the good old days, the horse and buggy days, the old, slow moving days!

I was born in David City, Nebraska in 1901 in a house without plumbing, running water, central heating or electricity. Two horses and a "surrey with the fringe on top" lived in a big barn on the back corner of the large quarter-block lot. There was a cyclone cellar at one side of the house; the privy and a chicken house were situated along the back lot line. We lived one block south of the Court House square and the Perkins Hotel (which was torn down just recently), where we took dinner almost every Sunday after church.

Several years after we had moved to Lincoln (1907), Dr. Beede built a large modern brick house where our cottage had stood. So I do not remember our little yellow and brown bungalow from the outside from our frequent return visits to David City. But I *do* remember it, mostly the inside. I can recall three incidents from my years there, although my mother used to say that I had been too young when they happened.

I remember when Irene fell against the baseburner in the living room, cut her eyelid and had to have five stitches. She carried that scar to her grave. There was another scar above her other eye, almost identical, which she got one year earlier as the result of a fall against the kitchen stove. Irene was accident prone, and she carried that tendency to her old age, too. I was six years old when she got the second scar.

I was nearly four years old when I cut off all my brother Ade's hair. Mother was expecting Irene, and unwisely said in my hearing, "I will have to cut off Adrian's curls when the baby comes. They are too much work." So the day Irene was born, I found the scissors and did the job for Mother. I even nicked his scalp in a couple of places. The only reason his yells were not heard was that I had taken him out behind the barn, and perhaps there was plenty of noise in Mother's bedroom. I haven't the faintest recollection of actually cutting his hair, but I can see perfectly how he looked when I had finished, and I remember how Mother took on when they finally had to tell her. The doctor fixed up the scalp cuts before he went home and my father got a barber to come downtown and open up his shop to give Ade a regular small boy's haircut. Somebody found the long curls where I had left them in the grass and Mother kept them in a candy box for many years. She used to show them to us when she told us that story.

When I used to tell my third recollection from David City, Mother always said that it never happened. I suppose that my father and I did not tell her about it. In the summer I was between five and six, I was sitting in the buggy out in the back driveway, holding a little bouquet of sweet peas in a small wine glass, probably watching my father curry-comb one of the horses. Father had tied the horse to a wheel (and this was some younger animal — not Fanny).

The horse jumped or pulled away and I fell out of the buggy and the wine glass was broken. This I *do* remember very well. I suppose I yelled, too, but Mother must have been away. And I was old enough to remember not to tell her when Father told me I should not. I had fallen on my head, so I wasn't hurt permanently.

These three memories add up to more than six years of my life in the town where I was born. I learned more about David City on our frequent return visits when we took the Columbus train from Lincoln in the late afternoon, stayed a week or so, and came back to Lincoln on the morning train. I used to take that same train to Lincoln when I was teaching (in Ulysses) until I bought my first Ford Model T in the spring of my first year there.

After my stories began to appear in Lincoln's *Sunday Journal and Star* "Focus" magazine in December 1981, some of my former pupils began to write to me and I have been invited to a Ulysses High School reunion in 1986. I was their class sponsor and coached their class play. At that time I knew those kids better than I knew my own family. I have renewed my

2

acquaintance with one member, when she came to a talk which I was giving in Milford (which had been announced in the paper in Seward, where she now lives). I plan to go to the reunion, if I'm still living in 1986. These plans for a very uncertain future are the main things that keep me going through the horrors of very old age.

In the spring of 1907, Mother took the three of us children, by train, of course, to western Minnesota to visit her parents who had moved there from Omaha three or four years before. We moved to Lincoln that summer and rented the house on R Street. I started to school in September.

One memory of my seventh year is another story I never told my mother. I was invited to join a group of neighbor children who were playing in the haymow of a nearby barn. I was usually too busy practicing my new-found and favorite art, reading, to join them. But on this day, I could not have had a new book, because I went to the haymow. I must have been a first-class prig (and no wonder, the way we were brought up), because I was profoundly shocked when I came upon a scene of semi-nudity. They were playing "Doctor" and I left them fast. It's a wonder that I didn't fall off the steep ladder onto my head again. I know Mother found out about the party, because she began to warn me about the dangers of such an affair.

That was her way. She never told me when she learned that I had done something wrong, she just forbade me to do it, ever, and went on for days about the dangers involved, so I never had to admit anything. If caught red-handed, I never admitted anything, either, and Mother would punish me without any discussion. That was her way, to ignore anything unpleasant as long as she could.

We moved to 130 South 28th Street in March of 1908, the day before my seventh birthday, and I remember everything quite well from then on. These memories divide naturally into two sections; from 1908 until I started my freshman year in high school in 1915; the second section covers the war, my high school days and the year I was sent away to college in September, 1919.

The first few years didn't change much. We had plumbing in both of our Lincoln houses, and two bathrooms in the second house. Both places had gas and electricity. People liked to hang onto at least one gas fixture in each room because the electricity was very undependable. Every storm would interrupt service and Nebraska's high winds were always blowing down a line somewhere. When we moved to 28th Street the houses just one block south of us did not even have city water piped in. There were streetcars and a majority of the larger houses had central heating. Stores, many larger buildings, and a few houses had steam heat but most furnaces circulated hot air up through floor registers. Often there were no registers to the second floor. This was warmed by the hot air that rose up the open stairway and sometimes by registers cut into the ceiling of the room below. Coal was universally used for furnaces with all the attendant features of coal delivery, smoke from every chimney and ashes to be carried out. Great plumes of smoke blew from the various power plants' tall chimneys, and curtains got very dirty fast.

Lincoln was really just a larger small town. The first good residential district had been east of the university and had spread to 27th Street by the time we moved in. The area south of O and west to about 25th Street had many nice large houses and the Near South district was pretty well built up by this time. We visited some people who lived near 19th and Washington and General Pershing moved his two sisters from the house three doors north of us to a new house which he built in the Washington area.

Sheridan Boulevard was put in about 1910, and houses began to be built along it and on the streets connecting it to South Street. Grace Pegler Marks lived with her family in a house on the north side of South, just where Sheridan took off to the southeast. She told me that her older brother Donald, then ten or eleven years old, was hired to turn on the beautiful new lights along Sheridan, using a switch across South Street from their house.

I don't know how street lamps in other parts of town were turned on at dusk. Perhaps they were some other type. Those near our 28th Street house were carbon arc lamps and hung only over each intersection. There were never any lights in the middle of the blocks. That is why we always played under the big light at 28th and N until we were called in at bedtime.

Omaha was quite a metropolis, but Lincoln was still just a small town. Most of Lincoln, but not all, had electricity, city water, telephones, and street-cars, and except for the last convenience, these were found in many of Nebraska's larger towns. The state was criss-crossed with branch railway lines, most every village had a depot and few farmers had to haul their grain many miles to a freight depot, so the banks and the elevators in the little towns were flourishing.

Out on the farms, however, people lived very much as they did in the nineteenth century. They had none of the town conveniences and were still farming with horses. Women carried in all their water from the well and then they had to carry it out again, so they were very stingy with water. There were no electric washing machines on the farm, even when I was teaching in small towns during the 1920s. Women had to work especially hard during threshing time in the summer.

"Thrashing crews" came with their big steam machines to one farm after another. Other farmers came to help drive wagons and pitch bundles. Their wives came to help cook the enormous noon meal and they were paid back by the other women when their turn came to feed the crews. I went to visit on a farm near Ulysses during the summer between my two years of teaching there. My hosts had the thrashers while I was there and I helped in the kitchen. It was the third week in July and, of course, there was no air

4

conditioning. We did some of the cooking on a kerosene stove on the back porch, but all the baking and some other cooking was done on the wood- or cob-burning range in the kitchen. I don't know how we stood it. It was hot enough out in the fields (I helped carry out lemonade to the men in the afternoon), but I believe the kitchen must have been twenty degrees hotter.

My host had a good automobile and someone went to town to buy ice cream for supper. I must have helped with the supper dishes, but all I can remember is falling into bed on the front screened porch and how exhausted I was. These scenes were exactly the same as farm life had been when I was a child. Nothing had changed except for the addition of the auto's trip to town for ice cream.

We drove around Lincoln with old Fanny and the surrey for two years after my father bought our first car in 1913. I am sure that he never drove that car, a 1912 or '13 Velie touring car, to work. Automobiles then, for most people, were for recreation only. We "went for a ride" almost every summer evening and on weekends. We just drove around town and for short distances into the country. The roads were still terrible and we never had the car out of the barn if it was cold or rainy. Father drove us once to camp at Crete, but except for that one trip of thirty miles or so, the Velie never was driven as far as ten miles from town. My grandsons, when sixteen, refused to believe that there had ever been a Velie (they were then complete authorities on all automobile lore). I had to spend some hours doing research in the library and bring home a photocopy of a 1912 Velie advertisement before they would admit that I knew what I was talking about.

That big red open car was the second one in our neighborhood. The first had been put together by a handy fellow who ordered the various parts from all over the country. Many of the first cars sold by dealers had been built in the same way. The Velie company had been carriage makers and the owner was the son-in-law of the proprietor of an old established firm which made carriages and wagons in Moline, Illinois.

We bought a seven passenger open touring car, a Buick, in 1915, and I learned to drive this one — it had a self starter. Cars began to appear in increasing numbers by this time — there were several in our part of our town — but not one garage. Cars went right into the carriage room of the barn, like ours. Twenty-eighth Street had been paved before the World War and a few neighbors put in driveways at this time. We already had one, which ran under a porte-cochere connected to one end of our front porch. Now people began to build garages, always on the back of the lot and often entered from the alley. One family built a garage so narrow that it was hard to put away the car because it had to be exactly in the middle so that the doors could be opened on each side.

Most young men were still taking their dates to downtown dances on the streetcar, and the young ladies carried their slippers in pretty bags over an arm. The few affluent men were still taking their dates to the Lincoln Hotel in horse-drawn cabs.

I graduated from the eighth grade of the old Elliott School at 26th and O and went on to four years in the new Lincoln High School. There were then no junior high schools. My youngest sister, thirteen years my junior, went to a *new* Elliott at 25th and N, then had three years at 26th and O Street Junior High (in my old Elliott School). The school board began to build separate junior high buildings around town and the eight year grade school four year high school system was gone forever.

The custom of steady dating came into fashion while I was in high school. Our American post-pioneer society had never been as strictly chaperoned and restricted as had been the older, wealthier groups in the eastern United States and in England. Our families did not have the retinue of maids which could spare one to accompany the young lady every time she went out of the house. On the frontier, girls had work to do—they grew up faster and were given more freedom. We in Lincoln went downtown alone and walked home from school and from parties with boys. The boys came in groups to the house when they were old enough, and sang songs around the piano or on the front steps. I was never exactly popular, but the boys came over because there was always something to do—a way to put in the evening, rather than to see me. And that was the pattern until about 1917. Perhaps it was the influence of the World War or of the family automobile, but "dating" began to be common and the old groups around the piano or on the front steps became less common. My mother was never happy with the "steady dating" and resisted it as long as she could. I was a senior in high school and seventeen before I was allowed out in the evening, except to be taken home from a party.

When I was in grade school, girls went in groups to parties, and there was no pairing off until the party was over. In high school, there were still mostly group parties until we were juniors and seniors. Even after most of us were allowed to date, some special plan was made for the evening; we went to a movie or to a friend's house to play the Victrola and dance (this went on several evenings a week at our house, with a very early curfew). Most parents, and mine in particular, were very fussy about homework and after our early supper we had to get busy with our books for at least an hour before we were allowed to receive any company in the front parlor.

On weekends we were allowed a little more freedom, but I never left the house before I had to go through the usual period of questioning. "Where are you going? What time will you be home?" And I had to be home by curfew time, usually seven o'clock, and there was trouble if I didn't make it. I wasn't allowed to stay out until midnight until I was in university. Then I was expected to keep sorority hours, which were very early in those days. Girls who came to stay overnight didn't get any more freedom because they were out in town instead of at the house. They liked Mother's food and the other rules were easy, but late hours were out. Even if we got home early and sat out on the front porch for a while, our vigilant neighbor to the south could see through the dark and hear through the vine on the porch, and she always reported to mother the next day. She could hear every remark made above a whisper.

We really didn't mind too much, we had been brought up this way and we didn't expect anything different. As the boys came home from service and began to go to college, things changed fast. Young people began to drink a little, very sub rosa, and a girl who was reputed to "drink" lost her reputation fast. You had to avoid the appearance of evil. You can believe it or not, but I was never in my dating life offered a drink of any sort. I didn't like beer and in my circles, nothing else was served. I never tasted "hard liquor" of any sort until I was married in 1929. I was probably the last girl of my generation to succumb to the new ways of doing things.

This chapter is a very brief description of my world in the first two decades of the twentieth century. I will have more to say about some aspects of this life in the chapters to come.

From left are Adrian, Irene, and Gladys in 1907.

HOLIDAYS OR FEAST DAYS

One of my first memories is the Christmas of 1907, when I was six years old. My cousin Edith, visiting us, acted as Santa Claus, and was doing a good job, when I, the eldest child spoke up. "Mama, that's just Edith." Of course, I remember the presents, the real lighted candles on the tree, and the photographer with his flash powder that filled the room with smoke. I remember the Fourth of July picnics and the shouting speakers.

But mostly, the holiday memories are of wonderful, enormous dinners. The meals were not really much different from our modern menus, but they were not quite the same. There was much more food and the food was richer—nobody had ever heard of cholesterol, and it was natural to gain weight as one grew older.

Recipes were apt to begin, "Take one pound butter, one pound sugar and 12 eggs. . ." Thick real cream was used in everything, and there was never just **one** dessert. Now I diet for weeks—trying to lose two or three pounds so I can eat a hearty Thanksgiving dinner.

Turkey for New Year's

New Year's was mostly an eating holiday. We always had turkey then, as we ate goose at Christmas. Thanksgiving was family reunion time and turkey. You went to Grandma's if you were lucky. We had no grandparents near us, but we did go every summer to visit my mother's oldest brother, who had children almost Mother's age and who lived on the family farm at Woodbine, Iowa, where she was born. We were often there over the Fourth, and I met Mother's old friend who was born July 4, 1876, and was named Independence Murphy.

Easter was colored eggs, church, new clothes and the Easter Rabbit. We did not hide eggs around the yard, but we enjoyed helping Mother with the dyeing. She always blew out the contents of the eggs, starting weeks ahead with every cake or omelet. These shells were lightweight, and you could make delightful heads, mounted on a collar of heavy paper.

8

We made our own May baskets, saving likely small boxes for months, or constructing them from cardboard. We would spend hours pasting crepe paper petals to make some beautiful creations. We made fudge to put in our May baskets. If we had transportation, we usually went out to Penn Woods (southwest of Lincoln) where we picked hundreds of long-stemmed violets to put in the baskets.

Firecrackers and politics

The Fourth was more firecrackers and political speakers than a big dinner holiday, but the dinners were very good. We did not have so many out-of-season vegetables and fruits then, and by July, the farm and garden bounty was in full bearing. We always had fried chicken and new potatoes and new peas in real cream. The dessert was strawberry shortcake. One year we visited a farm near Falls City—I was 12. I helped pick wild strawberries on a hillside near the river where the plants were thick and the fragrance met you before you came to the foot of the hill. We picked into lard pails and ate as many as we put into the pail. The adults did better and those shortcakes were served in big soup plates, with a large cup of berries and thick country cream.

My mother's only reference was the White House Cook Book. This was little changed since the 1890s. She did not serve those holiday menus in seven or eight courses, as they did, but there was almost as much food. She never served just pumpkin pie at Thanksgiving. There was always apple or cherry plus her specialty, lemon meringue pie.

Advance preparation

These dinners were not cooked and served by a small army of servants, as in the '90s. Mother usually had a "hired girl" who was treated as one of the family and ate at the table with us. On the big holidays, she usually ate at the second table, with the children.

There was always a lot of advance preparation for the large dinners, but Christmas took the most, as the house must be full of cookies and candy, in addition to the dinner. Mother started in October, when she made her fruit cakes and plum pudding. The mincemeat came next, and it was made with meat and brandy. The only strong liquor used in our house was for mincemeat and to soak the muslin cloths used to age the fruitcake and pudding.

These dinners were served around 1:30 p.m. (the evening meal was supper). At our house, we served only one meat, but we had friends from South Carolina who always presented a baked ham with their turkey. These hams were the old cure, which you soaked overnight, then simmered all the next day before baking them.

A typical menu might begin with oyster cocktail. Then with the turkey came a vast number of dishes. Two or three vegetables, both white and sweet potatoes, stuffing and gravy, salad and many sour relishes and sweet jellies and preserves for the homemade rolls. How could we have eaten any dessert? But we did, and I have seen some people take both pie and plum pudding at Christmas. We ate leftover pie for breakfast the next morning.

Leftovers for supper

For supper, we had leftovers, cake and fruit or ice cream. In between, children nibbled on cookies, stuffed dates and candy. I can't imagine how I can have such good teeth at the age of 82.

All of this food was prepared from scratch. The recipe for pumpkin pie began, "Cut the pumpkin in large pieces, stew until soft, drain and mash."

Pumpkin pie was made with thick cream and never served with whipped cream on top.

Those holiday dinners before the First World War were distant cousins of our modern meals, very overweight, and barely recognizable as relatives.

The Lincoln High School girls basketball team for 1919. First row, from left: Gladys Schaaf, Charlotte Kizer, Belle Farman, Alice Waite, Alex McNicol. Second row, from left: Grace Pegler, Cornelia Putney, ?, Elizabeth Wilcox, and Helen Wiggins. Photo courtesy of Belle Farman.

BEFORE RADIO AND TV

"But Grandma, what did you do all day?" my grandchildren asked when I told them these stories. We did a lot and had a very happy childhood. I remember back to my sixth year, in 1907, and I know we had plenty to do.

In the summer evenings the children living on 28th Street between M and O played every night on the corner at N under the carbon arc street light. Twenty-eighth Street was paved soon after we came, but there was very little traffic. Thirty-three kids between 4 and 16 lived in these two blocks, and most of them played at 28th and N: run, sheep, run; hide and seek; blindman's bluff; follow the leader; and many others. Parents began to call us in at dusk; some whistled, but one yodeled.

In cold weather, we played cards at the dining room table after homework was finished, usually with two or three neighborhood friends. Somerset, flinch and authors were popular. No one played with sinful poker cards. There were box games, very much like those played today, but they never were furnished with dice. Dice were also sinful. These games had a small arrow, mounted on a card, which you spun with your finger to indicate the number.

Crokinole board

We played checkers, and there was the big crokinole board. This was like a miniature pool table, with raised sides and netted pockets at the corners. It was played with wooden rings, which we shot with a finger, like marbles. The reverse side held the layout for some other game, and a box contained men for several games.

We always finished the evening with cocoa and often made candy; usually fudge, but sometimes molasses taffy—fun, but messy.

We subscribed to several magazines. I read St. Nicholas (for children), but also the adult magazines. The *Saturday Evening Post* and the *Ladies Home Journal* were delivered by a boy who collected the nickel or dime at the door.

11

We read a lot. Books filled the two sectional glass-fronted cases in the front hall, and I brought books home from the library at 14th and N — as many as I could carry. Our allowances were small, and I usually walked to save the nickel for carfare.

We never owned the phonograph with the big horn and the records on cylinders, but we listened to these at a neighbor's house. The big mahogany Victrola came for Christmas 1912, and then the other children came to listen to the large disc records. The machine would run down with a falling growl and someone had to wind it up again. We loved Harry Lauder and other comic singers, but we also listened to some good music.

I took piano lessons for years; no "nice" home was complete without a piano. I didn't practice enough but I was a very good sight-reader. Popular sheet music was very cheap, and the songs were made familiar by the vaudeville singers at the old Orpheum at 15th and O, where we went every week for years.

We sang: around the piano, on sleigh rides, hay rides and on the porch steps in the summer. Someone was always starting a song and we knew many. Everyone sat on the front porch; there was no air conditioning.

Birthday parties

Everyone had birthday parties. Popular gifts for a girl were sterling silver souvenir spoons and lovely little cup and saucer sets of English bone china. Each set then cost twenty-five cents. But I loved best the all-age family parties, which were held often in the winter. Everyone played in the games, and often there were forfeits for the losers. It was such fun to watch somebody's dignified grandfather get up and dance a spirited jig or sing a comic song.

Some parents forced their offspring to perform at these big parties, but ours were kinder; we never had to "speak pieces," except at school. Young ladies brought their music to these parties and left it with their coats upstairs until they were urged to perform. There were babies up there also, sleeping soundly on a bed fenced in by chairs.

We went to Capitol Beach almost every Sunday in the summer and were given 10 cents to spend each time. Drinks and rides were a nickel each. We finished with a picnic supper, and the best one was the annual Grocers and Butchers Picnic, when everyone was given a huge slice of watermelon.

And we went to the State Fair every year, but out there we ate a bountiful dinner at some church dining hall.

Lincoln, The Metropolitan Village

In many ways, Lincoln was a small town, although the population was 43,973 by 1910. Each summer we saw two circuses; Ringling Bros. and Barnum and Bailey were separate shows then.

12

Every Saturday morning for years, Dad took us out in the buggy to see the sights. We saw the circus unload, with the elephants pushing the parade wagons off the flatcars. We saw them set up the big tent about where Lincoln High School is today. We watched every parade in town. Every year we inspected the pumping station on A Street across from Antelope Park.

Best of all, we made an annual visit to the Fire Station at 23rd and O. In 1912 we were ready to leave when the alarm rang. My brother had just made his yearly slide down the brass pole from the dormitory above (girls were not allowed this pleasure).

We had seen the great horses, like the brewery horses one sees on television, tethered in such a way that they were free to run ahead when the alarm made the doors fly open. Dad pushed us out of the way and we watched the horses run to their places before the hook-and-ladder truck and the pumper beyond. The harness dropped down from the ceiling and men swarmed around, buckling straps and hooking up traces.

The driver sprang to his high seat and away they went, the firemen jumping on the vehicles anywhere as they rolled out. A man beside the driver clanged the big gong as the horses galloped east up the O Street hill, their enormous hooves striking sparks from the brick pavement.

This is probably the most vivid and exciting memory of my childhood.

THE BASEBURNER AND A HOT BRICK

One thing I DO remember from David City, before we moved to Lincoln in 1907, is the sight of the lovely glowing isinglass windows of the big baseburner that heated the front part of our cottage. The children dressed and undressed near its constant warmth and then went into the cold bedrooms, where a flannel-wrapped hot brick was a comfort to their feet.

I suppose our parents undressed there later in the evening, and hung their underclothes with ours on the big clothes-rack behind the stove. Daytimes, the rack held diapers drying and any small wash that was done between Mondays. Only on ironing days did the rack move out to be near the wood and cob range that warmed the kitchen. Baths were taken here, in the huge washtub, brought in from the back porch, which also held wood, cobs, and coal for the baseburner. Baths were Wednesday and Saturday nights in the winter and Mother scorned families who bathed only for Sunday. There were dark rumors about some people who sewed their children into their underwear for the winter. Well, the winters WERE very cold then (Doesn't everyone remember at least one childhood winter that was even colder than anything now-a-days?)

Scrubbing

And washing clothes was very different in the cold weather, when all the things had to be scrubbed on the board in the warm kitchen and then froze to the line immediately when hung outside. In very bad weather, lines were hung in the big kitchen overnight and the sheets and big towels hung there.

It was better and easier after we moved to Lincoln and had electricity and a washing machine and running water. And a furnace, with floor registers to stand over on cold mornings and to warm up after we came home from school. The upstairs bedrooms didn't heat very well, but they were not freezing.

14

The big square baseburner was a great advance in stove design. You filled a hopper at the top with small chunks of hard coal. This ran down to the fire below in the proper amounts and with the damper on for the night, would hold nicely until morning. Earlier stoves had been round, smaller and usually burned wood. They didn't hold very well through the night.

In those chilly bedrooms, there were many covers to keep you warm. We didn't have down comforters then, but we all slept on feather beds. They puffed up thick and billowed above a regular mattress which was used alone in the summer. Winter sheets were made of cotton flannel, always in double length. I suppose this was to keep the feet warm, but the great long things were hard to wash and hard to put on the beds.

All sheets were made shorter then; where we use a 108-inch sheet for a double bed, people used 90-inch sheets before the War. Mother made our everyday summer sheets, buying a bolt of heavy unbleached muslin in the proper width, and then hemming the sheets with the new treadle sewing machine.

Comforters

Above the feather beds, we had thick woolen comforters. I never noticed these earlier ones being made. But Mother gave me two when I was married in 1929 and the method was the same. I helped set up the quilting frame, which sat in the back parlour for weeks. Mother ordered the thick wool bats from a place near Des Moines. We quilted these between thin muslin covers, using a fine thin string and taking two-inch stitches. Then we tied this sandwich between pretty printed cotton covers with matching wool yarn. Finally we basted a nine-inch wide "protector" over the top end.

After we got electric blankets and furnace thermostats, I stored these wool comforters away for many years. But I dug them out of the cedar chest two years ago, threw away the worn covers and replaced the quilting. Mother used to send her wool bats back to the factory to be washed and recarded, but I don't know the address, so I ran mine through a cold wash and the dryer on cold air and they fluffed up nicely. With fresh no-iron covers tied on, they are now having a new life in my house, where we turn the heat down pretty low at night.

But now-a-days, no baseburner with its cheerful red windows sits in my living room anymore.

A PORCH AND A HORSE

We bought a house at 130 South 28th Street, not far from the east edge of Lincoln in 1907. This area around the small shopping center at 27th and O was then a very good residential district, with many large, well-kept houses. The streetcar ran to Wyuka (my father rode it home every day for noon dinner), and there were a few houses south of the cemetery across O Street, and then the farms began.

Tenth and O was the center of downtown and 11th Street was a fine wide avenue, running from old U Hall (University Hall, first building on the University of Nebraska Campus) on the north to a little south of the large fountain and basin at J Street, where drivers often stopped to water their horses. Our present suburbs were all separate and independent. Stores in College View (called Peanut Hill) remained closed on Saturdays and opened on Sundays, when almost every other store was closed.

Little traffic, little noise

There was very little traffic and little noise, except for the cries of the street vendors and the periodic rattle of the trolley cars. Everywhere children played in the streets.

Almost every house had a large porch in front, usually with a creaking swing and a few wicker chairs. Nobody had ever thought of a patio in the back yard, or of sitting out there during leisure hours. One sat on the front porch and watched what was going on. Front yards flowed together all along the block and it was not neighborly to put up fence. Most places had a few spirea bushes (called bridal wreaths) along the front porch and a round flower bed set into the lawn on either side of the front walk. These were usually planted with red cannas. Lawns were mowed by a reel hand mower and fertilized every other spring or so with horse manure. They had not yet thought of granular, odorless, chemical stuff in big sacks. There were plenty of horses.

16

The marks of the horse were seen all over town. There were horse troughs every few blocks and most places had a hitching post and a carriage mounting block in front. Our post was plain wood and I always coveted the one up the street — a little, black iron boy holding a large ring in his hand. Twenty-eighth Street was unpaved when we moved in, but in a few years they laid a concrete base and covered it with asphalt. All the children were entertained for weeks by this operation, especially when the steam roller came at the end. All stores delivered to the house and there were many street vendors. We loved Tony, the produce man, who shouted his wares louder than anyone else.

Use for an old piano box

There was a high board fence along the south side of our lot, (the only fence in the block). We (we because I always played with the boys if they allowed me) built a fine big playhouse against this fence. In those days all freight was shipped crated or packed in beautiful wooden boxes. Someone gave my brother two piano boxes, which had endless play uses. At the back door of stores, boys could usually find wooden boxes for the asking. Another year we dug a cave, quite large and much like the cyclone cellar in our David City yard.

We had a dog in the first years, but the little black mongrel got some incurable disease and had to be destroyed. Many dogs lived in the neighborhood and many others were always passing through. Collies were much the most popular breed and near us lived a bulldog, two Dalmations (we said coach dog) and one little fat pug. We played with them all and didn't miss our own dog.

There was a big apple tree out by the barn, fine for climbing, and supporting a swing for little children and a cherry tree up by the house. There was a small vegetable garden next to the barn in the back. We could "slide down the cellar door" (and get splinters) as there was an outside entrance to the basement with slanting doors.

Acquainted with the Pershings

We visited around a lot in the neighborhood and I often went to call at the Pershing home, which was then two doors north of us. If the general ever visited, I never met him, but Miss May Pershing, and her sister Mrs. Butler, were very good to me, and would even let me handle some of the fascinating oriental curios which filled the house.

Every lot but one in our block had a large barn out by the alley, which was "paved" only with ashes from the coal furnaces which many people dumped there. Our barn had two stalls, a carriage room and a haymow

17

above. The big barn door worked on rollers and there was a small door at the end for chores. Only three horses lived in all these barns — they were a lot of work. They had to be fed, watered, curried and the stall had to be cleaned out every day.

The garbage man would come in and carry your ashes out of the cellar and he would take away the sweepings from the horse's stall, unless you were saving these to put on the roses. I think we paid him $1 per month.

Fanny's pet goose

Fanny, our fat old horse had a dear friend, Pat, our big white goose. Some farmer friend gave her to Dad and we planned to fatten her for Christmas dinner. But she soon became a pet and died instead of old age, many years later. She lived in Fanny's stall and had to be shut up when they wanted to take the horse out for a drive. Pat really liked my father best and followed him around when he was home. She went down to the O Street corner twice a day, when he was coming home for meals. She knew when to expect him, and if once in a while she were late, she would run down the walk, honking and trying to fly with her clipped wings.

The goose hated the big red Velie and would attack it when it sat in the drive. When we finally put old Fanny "out to pasture" on a farm not far east of town, Pat grieved and mourned until we took her also out to the farm. For years, we used to drive out there several times each summer to visit them in the pasture.

Old Main at the University of Nebraska, the first building of the University which stood just west of the present Sheldon Gallery until 1949.

WOMAN'S WORK

Man may work from sun to sun,
but woman's work is never done.

Kitchen planning probably came in about the time Fannie Farmer revolutionized cooking with her new ideas about measurements and uniform recipes. Her first cookbook, published in 1896, became very popular in 1910. The houses we lived in had been built long before any kitchen planning. When running water and sinks arrived, some plumber installed the new sink, usually in a corner of the kitchen and much too low. I think the plumbers must have visualized filling a pail at the sink, or the very large teakettles then used.

There were few drainboards. Our 28th Street house had one of three in the neighborhood. Most women washed dishes at the big table which stood in the center of every kitchen and on which all work was done — *not* at a counter. The housewife filled the big kettle, put it on the stove across the large room, brought the water to a boil, then poured the steaming contents into the big dishpan on the table. There were no soap flakes or liquid soap, much less detergents. My Mother used a little wire box with a handle in which she put scraps left from used bars of soap from all over the house. This she swished back and forth in the hot water until she worked up a good suds. Sometimes she added a little cold water to the pan, but more often the water was much too hot and hard on hands. Many women added lye before putting in soap to "break the hard water," and this was even worse on the hands. Of course there were no rubber gloves for housewives.

By now another big kettle was boiling and was poured into another dishpan, to be used as a rinse. Mother spread a tea towel on the table at the left. First she washed the glasses, swished them through the rinse water, and turned them over on the towel. Then she washed the cups. Other dishes were turned over these to drain. When everything was dried, mother had to dump both big dishpans in the sink.

19

She only had to do this in David City. In Lincoln, there was a wooden drainboard to the left of the sink. There was no slant to this and no grooves to carry off the water, so here again she laid down the tea towel. These countertops were all wooden and had to be scrubbed with lye soap and a stiff brush.

A "Kitchen Cabinet"

I remember my mother-in-law's kitchen, which I first saw in the 1920s at the Douglass house in Plattsmouth. The usual low sink was in the middle of the south wall, all alone. The stove stood opposite on the north wall. On the east wall, between the pantry and bathroom doors, was a "kitchen cabinet" — a free-standing, movable piece of furniture and not a built-in cupboard. On the west, the big table stood in front of a wall of windows. All of these windows and the good light in this kitchen were most unusual.

At the table (not at the sink) vegetables were prepared, then taken back to the sink to be washed. Then a pan from the cabinet was taken to the sink, water was added to the carrots or whatever, and the pan was carried over to the stove. Think of the steps taken for every operation! This inefficient place was duplicated in every small town and on farms for years. Worse, many large houses had huge pantries which held the dishes and supplies and where much of the work was done.

Few women then had ironing boards on legs. An ironing board was simply a shaped, flat board. The large end rested on the kitchen table and the small end on the back of a chair; and in most homes, the iron had to be carried to and from the stove to be heated. More steps.

The only pans like our black iron ones to survive are some skillets of today. Mother had many iron pans, including a large kettle (with a bail — no handles) which she used for deep fat frying, and many baking pans. One big pan was a mold to make corn sticks like little ears of corn. Another baked twelve muffins (we called them "gems") in fancy fluted shapes. There were square and oblong iron pans used to make sheet cakes, though we usually had layer cakes, and to mold desserts.

Most sauce pans were made of grey enamel whose main disadvantage was a tendency to chip in use. Many women refused to use the new aluminum pans when they became available, because they thought the metal would cook off into the food.

A hole in a pan could sometimes be repaired by an itinerant tinker who came to the back door once a year or so. He would also sharpen your knives and scissors. The alley and back door traffic also included many tramps who would do any sort of work for a meal.

It was hard to get a carpenter to build anything new or different into a kitchen. The woman who had built our house — or rather she remodeled two smaller houses after putting them together — must have been very strong-minded. She had the sink set high enough (neighbors told us she had been very tall); she had one wall of counters with low storage space below; and she had a big cupboard built to the ceiling on the north wall. In the lower section of this there were two pull-out bins to hold flour and sugar. We used the bins often as mother made all the cakes and most of the bread we ate.

When we bought the house, the west wall of the kitchen held a huge stove which burned both coal and gas. The gas oven was above and the coal oven below, like any range. Mother replaced this with a large gas stove with six burners after a few years. Also, she soon had one of the new "fireless cookers" which drew their heat from pre-heated stone disks above and below a kettle. Now she could go out to an afternoon meeting and leave a stew or some soup safely cooking all alone.

There was a pull-out pastry board in the big north cupboard, but mother stored it in the "pan cupboard" under the counter and used it on the center table. She also had a marble slab she used for making candy.

Our corn popper was iron and so heavy that my father was the only family member who could pop corn. About 1912 he bought a new wire corn popper, which any of us could manage; and besides, we could see when the corn was done. In those days we bought our popcorn in the ear. Father rubbed one ear against another to "shell" the corn (strip the kernels from the cob). I never learned how to do this, so I was often upset when I couldn't find any corn ready to pop.

Father was also the only one who could use the heavy waffle iron. This sat up high on its base, so the whole iron had room to turn. He bought an electric one as soon as they came on the market, and our first one made four square waffles at a time. This was the iron mother used when she laid a piece of net on each square of batter for April Fool's breakfast.

No Place For Plug

I think an electric toaster was the first appliance we bought after the iron. It only toasted one side at a time, and to turn the slice you dropped the hinged side of the toaster so the bread slid down and turned itself over.

When we bought the 28th Street house in 1908, there was not a single wall plug in the place. The main rooms had chandeliers with gas burners turned up and electric sockets turned down. Other rooms had a single bulb hanging from the center of the ceiling. Most rooms had a bracket with a gas light, on one wall — as the electricity was always going off. After the new electric appliances came in, we had a double socket in the kitchen — with two more double sockets screwed into it.

We blew fuses almost every day. Finally, we had the house rewired, putting at least one wall socket in each room and several in the kitchen.

21

We were then all electric, except for the gas stove in the kitchen and one gas bracket in the upstairs bathroom.

By spring, houses got terribly dirty since they were all heated with coal furnaces or base burners. Spring cleaning was a painful effort which affected everyone in the family. Each one had to help as much as he could.

Carpet cleaning

All rugs and carpets were taken up and beaten outside (various school papers of the era are dotted with humorous items about boys beating carpets during their spring vacations). We hung the small rugs over a line to be beaten with the heavy metal carpet beater. Larger carpets were moved around over a coil bedspring on the ground so that most of the dirt fell out on the grass.

We hired a firm to take down the upper storm windows, wash the outside of the bedroom windows and put on the screens. My father struggled with the lower storm windows. He was not "handy" and he always required so much assistance that mother did all she could alone or with the help of a cleaning woman. Still, our storm windows were so long and so hard to handle that she usually got father to change these. I well remember the spring that he broke two of them in one season.

The curtains were washed and stretched in the back yard. This was one of the jobs which I always helped with. I also carried water for scrubbing walls and woodwork and threw up washing rags to someone on a stepladder. All woodwork and floors were washed with a strong lye cleaner, which was hard on the hands and soon ruined the paint or varnish. "Gool" Pavey, who died recently at the age of 99, was our painter and paper-hanger, and every other year he varnished or painted the woodwork. Mother liked to refinish the oak floors herself with shellac. She could work with a small brush along one narrow board at a time and she said it was "restful" work. In the four large front rooms downstairs, she only shellacked a narrow border around the large carpets, which were nearly full room size. Most of the bedrooms had only small rugs and had to be finished all over. A stock joke in the cartoons at this time always showed a man painting himself into a corner, but I don't think Mother ever did this.

Mr. Pavey always painted the kitchen and the bathrooms first as these rooms had been scrubbed the very first thing. He would abandon one of these and work on the woodwork in some other room as soon as it was ready for him. Mother always had to plan the order of cleaning very carefully so that time wasn't wasted. At last the carpets were laid and the furniture put back in place. All wooden pieces had been scrubbed and rewaxed. The beds had been taken apart and scrubbed and the mattresses aired in the back yard. We used old quilts for mattress covers then and these had been washed and replaced. Katie, our laundress, had been coming to us every day that she did not have a regular laundry job and there was often another woman who helped where needed.

When the windows shone and everything was finished, Mother went around putting new paper linings in the dresser drawers and on the shelves in the kitchen. Then she put doilies and dresser scarves back to cover up the wooden surfaces she had just spent hours waxing and polishing and she was done!

The annual nightmare

This is how it used to be when spring cleaning was an annual nightmare. About every four or five years in addition to the regular cleaning, we had to have new linoleum laid in the bathrooms and kitchen. Linoleum then was flimsy stuff which was only distantly related to the heavier, more durable floor coverings we are using today. The pattern was only printed on the surface and soon wore off in the traffic areas. It was easy to wear it into a hole, but we never let ours go that long. Mr. Pavey, who could do anything, probably put down the new floor coverings. During spring cleaning, we also had a new oilcloth cover tacked to the kitchen table. Also a large piece of oilcloth was always tacked to the wall back of the sink and drainboard. In those days, most kitchens and many bathrooms were built with a high dado or wainscot of dark wood, which showed water spots badly. It also darkened a room which had only one window. Whose idea can this have been?

We sometimes had to replace the rubber or composition runner on the stairway — we did not have carpet there. It seems to me that houses are much easier to keep clean now and of course, they do not get so dirty, since most people no longer heat with coal. Also we have more appliances to do the work. I am certainly delighted to see the passing of spring cleaning, as we knew it.

THE HIRED GIRL

When Bess Streeter Aldrich published the first Mother Mason story in 1918, the hired girl was still a fixture in many homes. Tilly Horn, Mother Mason's "girl," was a member of the family, hard-working, outspoken and much loved.

Young mothers especially needed help. Houses were large and there were few labor saving devices. No one had yet invented the profession of baby sitter. Since nursing homes were far in the future many of these big places also housed a grandmother or a maiden aunt who did some baby sitting and helped with the housework. Other mothers, not so blessed, took the children with them wherever they went.

My mother lived very far from any of her family. In David City, her eldest niece, teaching country school, stayed with us on weekends. She was a good worker and we all loved Cousin Edith. Another niece, attending business college later in Lincoln, was supposed to be helping Mother for her board and room, but she was terrible and Mother couldn't think how to fire her. She always had a date or had to study. My sister Irene and I noticed that she was sleeping in her room while "studying," so we were furious when we had to do the dishes. We also had to clean her room when she "had" to go down to school on Saturday. She got a job later, and lived with us for several years, paying board and room. Many families managed very well with a student on "board and room" but it never seemed to work out for us.

After my youngest sister was born in 1914, mother was a semi-invalid for five years, until she had the operations she needed. So we endured, or enjoyed, a succession of hired girls.

These came in several shapes, ages, colors, and ethnic backgrounds. The best "girl" and the only repeater, was Florrie, a black woman about forty years old — but she would not live in. Her family was grown and working, but Florrie would only help us during emergencies, as when the current "live-in" girl would leave us without notice. Florrie was the best cook we ever had. She would not change mother's cherished recipes (from the brown notebook), and several of her own dishes became permanent additions to our menus. We all loved Florrie and missed her until the next bad time.

After a month or six weeks, her cooking would suffer and her temper would get very short. We started keeping out of her way and Mother would sigh and start hunting seriously for a new "live-in" girl. Just before the new maid was to arrive, Florrie would clean furiously and make a lot of cookies. I think she loved us, but she wanted to be home, alone too.

These girls were always treated exactly the same, as members of the family who didn't wear uniforms and who ate with us at the table, unless company left no room. We kids often ate with the girl in the kitchen. In those days, all nice homes served every meal in the dining room, using white damask tablecloths and napkins. All women tried to keep house by the rules of Emily Post, and that is why the hired girl was needed so badly.

These girls always seemed to like us and often we liked them, but none stayed very long. Mother said it was because my sister and I ducked out of our regular chores and "took a vacation" when we had a girl. Perhaps she was right. Strange as it seems in modern times, none of our girls ever drank (as in Victorian novels). We never had any drink in the house, and who could buy liquor on $2.00 a week, room and board? The room was good, too; the big room with a good closet at the front of the house. I had to double up with Irene when we had a girl.

Mother had a friend whose girl, Bessie, came to her with the first baby and stayed until that daughter's own first child was born. She was called "Aunt Bessie" and was heard to say that she had "brought up" all the children.

Some of our girls left us for good reasons and after giving proper notice. There was a sick mother at home; Mary was getting married; Lizzie was taking a job in a store downtown. Mother fired very few—she would put up with almost anything. However, we heard her fire the girl who left us children alone in the house to go on a date. We went to bed and were all right, but we awakened to discover our quiet little mother had a temper and a loud voice, when needed.

The most abrupt leaving happened when our family came down with the flu in 1918. Our current girl went out the door right after the doctor, without taking any of her clothes. She came back after the scare was over to tell Mother how sorry she was. "I was just scared to death," she said. Our Florrie couldn't help us out in *that* emergency, as she had all her own family sick at her own house.

Many of our girls came back to see Mother and bring their babies to show her. They sent her Christmas cards for years, and one came to her funeral in 1969.

AUTOMOBILE ADVENTURES

We still used a horse and buggy for occasional transportation after we moved to Lincoln in 1907, when I was 6. My father rode the streetcar to work and home for dinner and supper. We usually walked.

In 1913, we acquired a "motorcar," a big red Velie. This was a large, stately machine, high off the ground. The driver sat on the right with the long levers coming up from the running board and the bulb horn at his right hand. There were no front doors. The huge brass headlamps were lighted with a match and fueled from a tank of acetylene on the left running board where there was also a tool box. There were carriage lamps on each side of the windshield and the hood was fastened down with wide leather straps. The ladies sat high in the back seat, wearing long linen dusters and veils tied over their big hats. We almost never had the top up because we seldom used this car in cold or rainy weather. One started the Velie with a crank, so I never learned to drive it.

Terrible driver

My father, like most men who learned to drive in their 40s and who were not mechanically minded, was a terrible driver. Also, he could never remember to check the oil or water, so there was often something wrong and we would have to be towed to a garage.

Alcohol was used as antifreeze and on cold mornings, Dad would take out a teakettle of boiling water and pour it over the manifold. (We bought quite a few new kettles because he often drove away with the one he had just emptied sitting on the running board.)

It was years before I got over the bad driving habits that I learned from my father. For instance, he taught me to throw out the clutch when going down a long hill. Luckily, I had stopped doing this, when, in 1918, I was driving my mother home from Omaha and we lost the right front wheel near the bottom of one of those steep hills on West Dodge Street. I was not driving fast (not with Mother in the car) and we were warned by two on-coming cars. These men honked and stood up and waved at us, and were were almost stopped when the wheel came off. Even so, it rolled a long way out into a field.

Foolishness

This car was the Buick, bought in 1915, and which I promptly learned to drive. There was no such modern foolishness as driver's licenses or age requirements. When you were tall enough to see over the wheel and could reach the pedals, you drove.

This Buick was a seven-passenger touring car, with a self-starter, a fixed top and side curtains. This was an advance, but it still had no windshield wipers or car heater. We put a great many miles on that car and I simply can't imagine how it stood up to our abuse for so long.

I walked to high school, as did almost everyone else; few young people were permitted to drive the family car. I was allowed to drive on many occasions and became the regular chauffeur for parties, school affairs, play rehearsals, etc. At 15, I would deliver my last passenger and then drive home alone. After I started to date, the boy would take me home in our car and then walk to his own house. About 11 p.m. one rainy night, my date was driving and, turning into our steep driveway too fast, ran into one of the pillars of the porte-cochere over the drive . . . (and in those days he had **NOT** had anything to drink). We had waked my parents, of course, and they came down in their robes and were really very nice about the whole thing. Dad even drove J home (after cocoa), because he was feeling pretty shaky and it was raining so hard.

Mother was still driving old Fanny with the surrey to club meetings, teas and other social affairs, but Fanny was getting very old and Mother decided she should learn to drive. So Dad took her out to practice and finally said she was ready to drive alone. So, one day she drove him back to work in the afternoon. We were never able to find out just what happened, but she drove home, parked the car just off the street and went to bed, where we found her when we came home from school. She refused to discuss her trip and she never did learn to drive, which she often regretted after my father died. Because Mother considered my brother a reckless driver, I usually was behind the wheel.

In the summer of 1918, we started for Omaha, where she was to attend a luncheon and we were to stay all night with a cousin. As we drove through University Place (then a separate town) we were arrested for speeding by the old traffic cop riding a bicycle. I was driving 20 miles an hour. We had to go at once to the police station and pay our dollar fine. Mother was late to her party.

There were few paved or gravel roads and it seems to me that it always rained when we stayed overnight in Omaha. We often got stuck in the mud coming home and it cost $3 to be pulled out. In the Platte valley near Ashland, one farmer kept a team harnessed up all day near his mudhole. You drove through deep powdery dust or deep mud or horrible deep ruts until the grader smoothed them out.

The first road markers were on the Lincoln Highway, later U.S. 30. They were smallish cards, tacked to telephone poles and easy to miss. Other roads had few signs. In 1918, we drove to Kearney to vacation on a ranch, taking along my friend Fern. Her young sister died suddenly, so we packed up the next morning and started early for Lincoln, It took us 16 hours. We had six flat tires, bought one new casing, several new inner tubes and patched several punctures. Those old patching kits came in handy and my brother was with us to help change tires, although Mother wouldn't let him drive. It was very hot and dusty and we had to stop in every small town for cold drinks. My youngest sister was only 4 and she always got car sick. The water pump gave out just west of Crete, and we were towed to town. We got a good rest and a fair supper there and started for Lincoln just before dark. But then I got lost. There were few markers on that road and I was so tired I couldn't see very well. What does that trip take now — three hours?

Cars were more interesting and individual in those days. You could never mistake a Pierce-Arrow for anything else. Many people bought steamers and a few had electrics. My "steady," J, and I used to go on double dates with B.L. who could borrow his aunt's luxurious little electric coupe, with flowers in the cut glass vases.

Soon the Model T began to be seen everywhere and the world had changed, never to be the same again. I am happy to have lived through these early days of life of the "horseless carriage" and I had a wonderful time.

There is no record of the number of cars registered in Lancaster County in 1907, because the county did not keep any record. In those days and for some years after, you wrote to some official at the Statehouse, saying you had bought this automobile. They entered your data in a ledger, by hand, giving you the next number in the list. Then they sent you this number and you had a license plate made of any material at hand, sometimes leather. The state began supplying plates in 1915.

In the 1920s, when they added prefixes to the license numbers, Lancaster County was second in the number of cars, so the counties were then keeping count. Custer County was fourth on the list then.

WASHDAY WAS EXTENDED

Washday began Sunday night, after supper. Mother went to the basement and put the white clothes to soak. In the kitchen, I sat down and shaved a cake of Fels Naphtha soap into thin flakes. Mother then simmered this soap all evening in water and finished with a pan of soft soap.

The soaking was done in the big wooden tub of the new electric washing machine. The laundry room was large, floored with brick and furnished with two deep laundry tubs and a two-hole gas plate mounted on a bench. There were two square tin tubs for rinsing, and sections of garden hose were attached to the faucets for filling the tubs and the boiler, one of those beautiful long copper affairs.

Mother later had a mania for getting rid of "old" things. We weren't able to find the copper boiler when she sold her place; she probably gave it to the junkman for 50 cents.

Up at 5

Mother was up at 5 a.m. on Monday, filling the boiler, starting it to heat over the gas, wringing the clothes out of the soak water, getting them into the boiler and adding the soft soap. (What a blessing the electric wringer was!) Sunday night she had rubbed soap into any spots she found, using a half-size scrub board, which was usually kept in the kitchen for small hand wash.

Katie arrived promptly at 7 a.m., coming from North Bottoms by streetcar. We visited her several times — she was our laundress for many years and a good friend. She came to my wedding. She lived just beyond the 10th Street viaduct in one of those gleaming little white cottages surrounded by a low, white picket fence. This area was then called Russia Town (pronounced *Roosha*). Katie never walked; she trotted. If things were not ready for her, she grumbled and complained all morning; so they usually were ready.

29

As soon as the first load was on the line and the second load in the rinse tubs, Katie came up the inside cellar stairs for coffee — and that had better be ready, too. Mother always had homemade coffeecake, which she baked between starting the boiler and getting our breakfast.

In the summer, by the time the last things were out on the line and the laundry room cleaned up, the first things were ready for the iron. We did the flat ironing on the big kitchen table, padded with a blanket and an old sheet. The ironing board did not have any legs; the ends were propped on the table and the back of a wooden chair. The first iron was the heavy one, with the handle cast in one piece and padded heavily with a piece of blanket. Better was the two-piece iron, with a removable wooden handle. You kept one or two irons heating on the stove while you ironed with a third. To test the iron's heat, Katie picked it up and touched it with a wet finger, then rubbed the iron with a thick cloth pad.

Katie had dinner with us, admiring the gleaming white cloth and the big napkins that had been washed the week before. I think she had her own napkin ring.

Piled up

Back to the ironing after dinner, and the flat things were piled up on the counters and the table in the pantry. Sometimes (very seldom) she got everything done and put away before she went home. But in the winter, when things froze on the line and took longer to dry (frozen long underwear flapping), she helped Mother with mending or some special cleaning job.

Here is where I come in. We had an electric iron by the time I was old enough to help. I learned on napkins and handkerchiefs (dozens of these; remember, no Kleenex). The big linen napkins were sprinkled very wet and had to be ironed until nearly dry on the wrong side, then polished on the right. It seemed to me the ironing went on all week. *Everything* had to be ironed.

'For company'

After I was married, I finally talked Mother into *not* ironing the tea towels and Turkish towels. But she always ironed a few and kept them in a special drawer "for company." Young people, say a special prayer every day for automatic washers, dryers and no-iron fabrics!

BAKED BEANS ON WASHDAY

Before the First World War most housewives did not serve as great a variety of foods as they do today. Few vegetables and fruits were shipped in out-of-season — you ate strawberries every day when you could — homegrown and 10¢ a quart. Most women served the same meat on the same day each week; after all, in 1907 we were only a generation away from the pioneers who had lived in sod houses and who ate boiled beans, bacon or salt pork, bread and coffee three meals a day every day — with dried apple pie now and then.

Our food was varied and good. Mother repeated a few favorite menus often, but seldom on the same day of the week. And we almost never knew what we could find when we came home to noon dinner. Except for baked beans and Boston brown bread on washday. I don't know how this custom came to be; perhaps in the David City days, when the boiler sat on the range all morning, this was a good time to have beans in the oven. There was *always* chicken on Sunday. This wasn't just the title of a book published in the 1940s, but a fact of life in the 1910s. Also chicken was usually the food served at parties. You had creamed chicken on biscuits, chicken salad, chicken pie and delectable pressed chicken molded in its own broth.

A Dollar for a Roast

In the summer, Mother sent me to do the grocery shopping at Towne's store at 27th and O Streets. She would tell me, "Get a dollar pot roast." This would be a four pound chuck or rump, cut off the big piece while you waited. Or I bought round steak, cut and sawed off the whole round. Or pork chops, all cut at once and then each piece chopped off. Chicken fried round steak was a favorite supper dish, especially if there were no leftovers from dinner. When the men came home after 5 o'clock on the streetcar, they would walk up 28th marching to the beat of the round steak being pounded for supper in half the houses.

31

About 1915, my Aunt Jo came from New York to visit us for two weeks. She learned that Towne's butcher did not carry sirloins or T-bones, so she ordered some thick T-bones and broiled them in the gas oven. My father cut into that beautiful, juicy, pink steak, and shuddered with horror. My mother took it back to the kitchen and cooked it to a very well-done state — and then he said it was dry. No wonder.

Aunt Jo, full of new ideas from the big city, introduced us to vegetables served in something other than thick white sauce, as was usual. We had new peas in real cream, often with tiny pink new potatoes; cauliflower in cheese sauce, also made with cream; and baby carrots cooked with butter and brown sugar. Too sweet (called candied carrots), but we *would* eat them — much better than with that thick white sauce. Father rejected broccoli, which Aunt Jo went all over town to find, after one bite and asked Mother to get him some canned tomatoes.

Almost every morning, mother baked one or two pies, a cake twice a week and cookies often enough to keep the cookie jar full. After I grew old enough, I took over the cake and cookie job, as I loved to cook and Mother was very good at letting me get in her way, and Father would eat anything I made, without his usual carping remarks.

None of us was fat, although we ate two or three slices of home-made bread at dinner, with butter and jam or jelly. Nobody dreamed of eating a naked slice of bread. Father was a very big man, 6 feet 4 inches tall and 200 pounds, but he was not fat. Mother was very thin until her late forties, but then *she ran* off all the calories she ate and I suppose we children did, too.

Mother baked bread once a week, usually on Friday, when she often made a thick vegetable beef soup, which simmered all day while the kitchen was warm and the oven was going, and we all fought for the heel of a warm loaf at supper.

The only casserole we had was macaroni and cheese, and meat loaf was the only dish we made with ground beef. The butcher ground this for you in his big machine while you waited. Before we got the meat grinder that clamped to the kitchen table, Mother chopped her cooked beef for hash in a big wooden bowl. This was never used for salads and the chopper had a double blade rounded to fit the bottom of the bowl. Hamburgers were never made at home until the 1920s — you ate them and hot dogs at baseball games.

Preparations on Sunday

The baked beans were soaked all day on Sunday, boiled briefly and put in the big brown beanpot, ready to bake early Monday morning. Mother added a big chunk of salt pork, brown sugar or molasses and some of her own catsup to the pot and part of the soaking liquid. This went into the oven before breakfast on Monday morning and was ready for dinner at noon.

The brown bread was steamed in several one-pound baking powder cans, greased and filled to two-thirds of their depth. This was steamed with the lids on for two or three hours before dinner. The mixture contained three kinds of flour: often whole wheat, cornmeal and Grapenuts, my Father's favorite cold breakfast food. This was all mixed with molasses, sour milk, soda, and a cup of whatever was on hand: raisins, nuts, or chopped dates. After baking, this bread was turned out of the cans and cut in pretty round slices. I haven't tasted Boston brown bread or even thought of it for many years.

We ate about six meals a day: always a snack after school and at bedtime and in the morning during the summer. Now I weigh only five pounds more than I did at eighteen and I don't know how I have survived with such good health at 82. But wasn't it fun?

DOWNTOWN BEFORE THE 1920s

Downtown looked very different when we moved to Lincoln in 1907. The Burr Block at 12th and O, six stories high, was known as the "skyscraper." Most buildings were three stories or less. I do not remember the skyline as much as the sidewalk or "child's eye" view. This was very different from today.

The sidewalks were punctuated with areaways which held stairs, leading down to stores in the basement, and with gratings that covered small freight elevators. Women wearing the high heels that were almost universal when they went to "town" had to watch out lest a heel catch in one of the gratings. If a delivery was being made, one had to walk around the raised gratings and the elevator, and usually there was very little room.

Several buildings had their first floors built up above the sidewalk level, so you had to climb five or six steps to reach the front doors. As far as I know, the Burr Block, where Cliff's is today, has the only remaining sidewalk stairs. These buildings were built in the monumental style of late Victorian architecture. At that time, large buildings were supposed to have important looking entrances. This meant designing an important surrounding for the front door. This might be an arch, or pillars, or both, but always there were several steps up to the door. One writer said an entrance without high steps looked "like a face without a chin." There used to be another high stoop like this at 13th and O, where Penney's is today. On the west, or 13th Street side, there were several areaways with steps leading down. One that I remember led to a shoe-shine parlor-repair shop. Another provided access to a barber shop, marked by a red and white striped pole on the sidewalk above.

This was the United Cigar Store building, and the next building east was the Wonderland Movie Theater—probably the only theater ever in town without a restroom (when one needed, one went to the Cigar Store building next door). Many of the early movie houses were placed in a regular narrow store space, with a level floor unchanged except for adding seats, a piano, and a screen. I don't think I ever saw a movie at the Wonderland.

At the YMCA, at 13th and P, raised entrances opened to steps that led up to the main floor. There was a mid-sidewalk stairway down on the 13th Street side; it led to areas under the sidewalk and building; these included a men's "comfort station," barber shop and bowling lanes. The "Y" swimming pool, then one of the few public pools in town, could not be reached from outside. One went up the front steps to the lobby, then down a long, narrow inside stairway to the pool area. Once I was taken there to see a swimming exhibition (my brother was taking a swim class). This was the first time I ever saw any diving from a springboard.

Shining shoes

These days, and through the 1920s, we were always getting our shoes shined, and every time I could spare a nickel I had mine done. It must have been fun, as I am quite sure I didn't care that much about how my shoes looked — and we did have a shoeshine box at home that we were supposed to use. For a shine at the YMCA, one walked down the steps and into a long and narrow subterranean area with the shoe repair section at the back. On the right were three large built-up steps along the wall. On the top step was a long row of chairs, usually full of customers. In front of each chair, two metal footprints rose up from the next lower step to show where to place one's feet. The shoeshine operator stood on the last step. In front of the first three or four chairs there was a heavy green curtain arranged to form the partial enclosure that was the ladies section. The curtain hid ankles from the gaze of anyone passing by or sitting in the row of armchairs along the left wall, where customers awaited their turn.

The bootblack (and he usually *was* black) did a fine job. First he cleaned the shoes, then applied polish with his bare hand, and finally finished the job by using a long narrow polishing cloth to put on the shine. After several passes he would loudly snap the cloth. I didn't ever tip him, as I didn't know any better. I learned about tipping when I took a Pullman trip overnight when I was eighteen.

You can still see one old areaway and steps down to the basement on the 12th Street side of Cliff's, and there you can also see the original wall of the old Burr Block (today's Anderson Building). In the sidewalk west of Magee's on 12th Street, you can see one of the few remaining sidewalk elevators. Many store basements were excavated out under the sidewalk, usually with a grating covering a small elevator for freight deliveries.

Downtown floods

Salt Creek, overflowing the serpentine bends that marked its pre-channelization course along the west side of the railroad yards, flooded its valley after almost every hard rain. Even such downtown corners as 13th and O were subjected to flooding, thanks to the inadequate storm sewer system and heavy downpours. The street would fill up, then the water would overflow sidewalks. It had to run into basement areas where outside steps and freight elevators opened onto the sidewalks.

I remember many individual stores. Farquhars, our neighbors when we Schaafs lived on 28th Street, operated a clothing store east of 13th on the south side of O. At the end of this block was the Lincoln Candy Kitchen, run by Alex Keriakedes (I remember a taffy pulling machine in their window). Across the street to the north was the Acme Chili Parlor. Farther east, at 16th, was Piller's Drug Store, the regular hangout when I was in High School.

It seems to me there was a drug store on nearly every corner. Each had its elaborate marble soda fountain and the drug store mark of two huge jars of colored water in the front window. At them, one could buy a cardboard bucket of ice cream. Our family always bought these at Rubendahl's at 27th and O. This place soon became Taylor's Drug. It was a hangout for nearly everyone from the old Elliott School. Even better remembered though, is Harley's Drug at 11th and O. Fern Jackson and I used to go there after school, as her boyfriend of the time was the "soda jerk." I'm sure he didn't cheat the store . . . much!!! However, he may have slipped us a few extra nuts on our chocolate-fudge nut sundaes!

We bought most of our groceries at Towne's, across the street from Taylor's on O Street. Towne had a butcher shop in his store, but most grocers did not. The meat shops usually were separate and looked very different. Against the walls hung sides and haunches of meat. The butcher, who always wore a hard, straw hat, cut one's order from these on a large butcher block table in the middle of the store. There were no ready-made cuts and no showcases to put them in. Fish and fruits and vegetables were often sold in separate stores. Heitkotter's, on South 10th Street, was *the* place for fish, and there was a fine fruit store at 10th and P.

At first sight, hardware stores looked much the same as today. Obviously, there were no power tools and very few electric appliances.

Many of the small stores had molded tin ceilings, embossed with elaborate designs and then painted. Also, many houses had such ceilings in kitchen and bathrooms, as did ours on 28th Street.

Stores on the move

Most stores moved around downtown a good deal — probably looking for the ideal spot to settle down. The two grocery stores on N Street and the one on O Street east of 14th never moved. Lawlor's, for instance, moved several times before they finally settled down near their present location on O Street east of 11th. Their original store was where Hardy Furniture Company later built their own big store (in the building at 1314 O, now occupied by Commercial Federal).

I particularly remember the early Miller & Paine store, at the firm's present location, when there was only the first two-story section on the 13th and O corner — before the eight-story addition to the west was built in 1916.

The store was long and narrow and the interior was typical of department stores of its day. Hanging from the ceiling were the lights and big fans. All of the stores got very hot in the summer. The most noticeable feature of most stores of the time was the use of change baskets which traveled on a network of wires that criss-crossed below the ceiling and led to a little balcony office back in a corner. There were no cash registers in the individual departments. A clerk put a large bill and the sales slip in a small metal basket and pulled a long cord which hung from the wires. This raised the basket onto the cable network, rang a bell and sent the basket whizzing along the wires to the balcony office. There a teller would count out the change, prepare the customer's copy of the saleslip and send those items whizzing back to the point-of-sale in that remarkable basket. Its arrival rang the bell again and a tug on the dangling cord dropped the basket down to the level where the clerk would then hand the customer her (or his) change along with the package containing the purchased merchandise.

When Miller and Paine built the tall addition, the basket system was replaced by pneumatic tubes that carried the transactional papers and money in small metal cylinders. This system centered in an office behind a grille in the store's basement.

Need for a man

Many people still living can remember Calvin Edwards, the very tall, slender floorwalker on the main floor. If trouble developed with the pneumatic system, a signal to Mr. Edwards would send him hustling down the stairs to the basement and soon he would come back with whatever was needed.

Sales departments then looked quite different from those of today. Few items were out on display. They were kept in drawers instead. There was very little self-service. The customer sat on a stool in front of the counter and the clerk looked in a drawer for the item requested.

In the boom of the 1920s, many taller buildings went up as banks and stores expanded and the old downtown vanished. Blocks were soon filled up from corner to corner and soon one could no longer find a three-story building next to a small wooden shack . . . not anywhere . . . not anymore.

TWO TELEPHONE COMPANIES

When we moved into our second Lincoln house in 1908, there were two telephones in our dining room. My father had gone into the real estate business, and to reach all his customers he had to subscribe to both phone companies. One was the Bell Company which had a stranglehold on the exchanges of most of Nebraska. The other company, established in Lincoln in 1904 as the Western Union Independent Telephone Co. was owned and managed by Lincoln residents. It was fighting hard against the spreading Bell monopoly. In 1905, the young company changed its name to the Lincoln Telephone Company (Telegraph was added later) and opened its offices in Lincoln with 1,800 customers and 2,450 phones. The company's new president, young Frank H. Woods, was fighting for the life and survival of the infant company. One of its greatest assets was the automatic dialing system, one of the first in the country and the first successful one in Nebraska.

In our dining room the new "candlestick" type phone sat on a low table and we children soon learned to use the dial and make a few calls.

The other phone — the Bell Company's — hung on the wall with a footstool below for children's use. It was a large oak box with a mouthpiece near the top, a cord and attached receiver on the left and a crank handle on the right. To initiate a call, you picked up the receiver and turned the crank. A voice inquired "Number, please."

Telephone manners

At first, most people did not bother to look up numbers, but would say something like: "I want to speak to Mrs. Jones on East M Street" and Central would ring the proper number. Mother would not let us do this and we soon learned proper telephone manners. Eventually most other people did the same.

The old ways survived in small town and country exchanges for years. Everyone knew the operator (the exchange was often right in her home) and she knew everyone. She knew who had gone to Omaha for the day and that someone else was away on a two week vacation. She knew when a post-operative patient was well enough to have visitors and she also knew a great many things she did not tell about the townspeople. All country phones then were on party lines and when someone answered a farmhouse phone, Central could hear receivers coming off their hooks all along the line. Someone might even cut in on a call once in a while.

The small Lincoln company struggled against mighty Bell for years and finally won the fight in southeastern Nebraska. Bell moved out of Lincoln and took over virtually all of Nebraska north of the Platte River and/or west of Grand Island. Lincoln Telephone bought out the other independent companies in southeastern Nebraska as well as acquiring the remaining Bell properties in that area. Business prospered and the total number of telephones in the Lincoln company's area soon rose to 42,370.

It was in 1912 that Lincoln Telephone Company formally took over and Bell moved out. Lincoln Telephone absorbed all of Bell's Capital City employees who did not move from Lincoln. The changeover was so friendly that a large joint dance was held in April 1912 to mark the occasion. At this time, there were 14,724 phones in Lincoln and of these, 1,211 had been served by both companies. The telephone book was much thicker and numbers were changed. Ours was 1014 in 1908. Over the years, it changed to 2 – 1014, then to HE2 – 1014 and finally, when mother sold her house in the 1960s, it had become 432 – 1014.

In 1905, the Bell company put up a building at 130 South 13th Street, today occupied by the Exchange Restaurant. This old Lincoln landmark has three stories and an outside stairway on the alley. Now that the "new" front has been removed, it looks very much as it did in my childhood. I knew this building well; after Bell moved out, my father rented the first floor for an office. The long room, which had been lined with operators in their white shirtwaists and pompadours, was now lined with roll-top desks and old fashioned big typewriters. The typists still wore long dark skirts, white waists and pompadours. Except for a private office at the rear, the place was one big room, with two huge windows in front and several half-round windows high on the north wall.

I don't think there were any metal files — I remember long lines of cardboard file boxes on shelves behind the desks. Somewhere near the back was the fascinating copying machine. It looked a little like the first small printing presses with a large metal wheel on the top. This was turned to bring pressure on the letter to be copied, which was resting on the flat bed below. As in many offices of the era, shaded light bulbs dangled on long cords from the high ceiling.

Before he moved into the Bell building, Father had an office in the large two-story building a little south on a site occupied today by the Lincoln Benefit Life Building. We walked up a high stairway off 13th Street to reach the office, and when we left we often walked down a long dog-leg hall to the back stairs, then out to N Street on our way to the old Carnegie Library at 14th and N.

Meanwhile, the Lincoln Telephone and Telegraph Company was steadily growing. For years the company rented quarters for exchanges and offices all over town. Then L T & T built the Automatic Exchange Building on the alley between M and N on the west side of 14th Street. In 1914, a large new place was constructed on the corner of 14th and M to serve as company headquarters. The company also built several smaller buildings on sites around town to house automatic dialing equipment. Construction also included a storage building at 21st and L (and by now there are several big L T & T buildings at that location). In 1949, the company erected the first unit of the present office and equipment center at 15th and M Streets — a telephone center since enlarged and a tower added.

Not only in building has the Lincoln company kept up with the times, L T & T has been an industry leader in research and development of new improved methods and equipment. Among these are burying the lines in country areas and working out the direct dialing system for long distance calls.

The 15th Street building houses a wonderful museum of old telephones and related historical items. Although not the largest such museum in the country, it is considered one of the most complete. Don't fail to see it. And remember that in 1907, when some of these old phones were in use, the strong vigorous Lincoln Telephone and Telegraph Company of today was just a little fledgling firm fighting (and beating) the great Bell.

The old Lincoln Telephone & Telegraph Building on the northwest corner of 14th and M Streets.

A YOUNG MOVIE FAN

My father was stage-struck all his life, and I seem to have caught his interest. From about 1910 to 1915, as I remember, he took all of us to the vaudeville show at the old Orpheum every Friday night (no school the next day). I don't know why we stopped doing this. Perhaps the first World War led us to other activities, or perhaps the general slowdown of vaudeville over the country cheapened, or reduced the shows at the Orpheum.

When Bertram Goodhue, the architect, was here on one of his inspection trips while the new capitol was being built in the 1920s, he looked north up 15th Street and saw the Orpheum blocking the view in that direction — the building stood on the north side of O Street, in the middle of 15th and facing toward the capitol. Capitol architect Goodhue suggested that 15th be opened to R Street, a fine building put up there and 15th made into a mall with a beautiful prospect from the capitol. The Orpheum eventually moved to a new building at 12th and P Streets, where it showed movies and a few vaudeville acts. The theater at 15th and O became a movie house, the Rialto. This building was torn down many years later when 15th was opened to R Street. And the State Historical Society Building there fulfilled Goodhue's plan.

When I was attending the University of Nebraska in the 1920s, I saw a few movies and some university productions at the new Orpheum, but there were no full bills of vaudeville at that time.

Passes to a movie house

During the war, my father invested in a company that owned some of the new movie theaters. He didn't like movies and seldom saw any. But we children were given passes to the movie house which stood where the Stuart Theatre is today. This was then called the Lyric. This house showed the badly photographed, badly directed, jumpy first movies — silent, of course. I was usually there every Saturday afternoon and saw many of those terrible old films.

41

I remember especially a serial which went on forever, "The Perils of Pauline," with Pearl White as the star. Each episode left her in some dreadful danger: tied to the railroad track with the engine approaching, hanging from the high bridge over the river, or locked in the bank vault. And we had to wait a whole week to learn how the hero would rescue her.

That was why I had to be there every Saturday.

The dialogues and the sub-titles were flashed on the screen—this was many years before the "talkies." A woman played appropriate music at a piano in the orchestra pit. Small boys in the theater also accompanied the movie with loud comments and with boos and kissing noises in the more tender moments.

Long feature pictures

I saw cowboy shows as the movies got better and a few fairly good long feature movies.

Among these were Lilian Gish in the "Birth of a Nation," Mary Pickford in "Pollyanna," the Keystone Cops with their wonderful chases in a beat-up Ford, Douglas Fairbanks in the "Three Musketeers" and later, Rudolph Valentino in "The Shiek." I also saw every picture with Charlie Chaplin starring. I didn't like the romances, as it was terribly embarrassing when the silly courting dialogue was flashed on the big screen.

One of the best parts of the early movies was the newsreel, shown after the main feature. This was at a time when magazines did not have many photographs or illustrations, long before *Life*. The scenes shown in newsreels were much like the TV news today, the big disasters and the annual spectacles such as the Rose Bowl parade, the Easter and Christmas parades in New York and the Mardi Gras in New Orleans. If there was no big disaster or celebration to be shown, the newsreels would fall back on stock pictures.

There was almost always a shot of the navy, especially the great battleships, steaming along in line. Another favorite was a sequence of the enormous guns firing in practice from various coastal forts. The recoil was incredible. Steeplechase races from England were popular, and there was an occasional polo game. There weren't nearly as many sports events then as we see nowadays on television, but we usually saw the President throw out the season's first ball at the Washington baseball game.

Until I was old enough to have dates, I usually saw the shows with another girl, although a 14-year-old female was perfectly safe in these early movie houses. I outgrew most of my early craze for movies as I got older—I think I have seen only two movies in the last 30 years. But if there had been any vaudeville as I grew up, I would have been there.

Best seats: Balcony Row 1

At the old Orpheum, our seats were always in the first few rows of the balcony, not much cheaper than orchestra seats below, but much the best place to see and hear. My hearing was better then and we heard and understood every word of the dialogue and the songs. There were then no microphones or amplifiers; if I had any voice left, I could still sing you the news-of-the-country topical patter song of the popular Gallaghar and Shean. "Oh Mr. Gallagher, oh Mr. Gallaghar." "Well, what's on your mind this morning, Mr. Shean." "I think something must be done, bout the way this country's run." "I think you're right in what you're saying, Mr. Shean." Vaudeville had everything — animal acts, acrobats, magicians, comics alone (now called stand-up comics) or in pairs. Songs, dances, sections of popular plays or from Shakespeare and other classics.

By the time I saw vaudeville, the material had been cleaned up and no longer much like the tough, bawdy, for-men-only sort of shows which had prevailed in the 80s and 90s.

We saw Sarah Bernhardt on several of her "farewell" tours. She played entirely in French, but her voice was wonderful. On one of her last appearances, after she had lost a leg, she played the entire show reclining on a sofa. I think this was an act from "L'Aiglon," but with the sofa, perhaps it was "Camille."

I saw a lot of junk, of course, but also some very fine actors and singers and I don't think my time was entirely wasted. One friend near my age told me that her career in classical dance was motivated when we saw Ruth St. Denis and her dancers at the Orpheum.

Sunday performance question

I've been reading a book on the history of American vaudeville. It says that most variety theaters were open seven days a week, but I don't think that the Orpheum played on Sunday. Lincoln was a very churchy town then, and my sister Irene once was a model in a charity style show on a Sunday at the Orpheum. This was in the early 1920s and perhaps the place was then closed and getting ready to move to 12th Street. Irene was a tall, thin model type and she walked across the stage, leading a huge white Russian wolfhound.

After the Lansing Theater at 13th and P Streets became the Oliver, I saw several legitimate stage plays there. "Uncle Tom's Cabin" came once every year, of course, and there were some other perennial favorites. But what I remember best was a summer when a stock company played there for three months. They fascinated me, and as I had acted in several high school plays, I could never figure out how they could produce a **different** play each week. I went to a matinee almost every week and balcony seats were very cheap. I never sat in the highest balcony, where seats were only a nickel.

The movies, the radio and TV ruined vaudeville, although it survived a few years playing two or three acts between the shows of a movie house. Most books use 1932 as the year when vaudeville collapsed altogether. Some

43

of the best artists survived by going into the big New York musicals like the Follies, which came out with a new show every year. Fred Allen and Will Rogers were among these. Some became popular radio stars later.

Remember Fred Allen, Allen's Alley and Senator Claghorn?

Of the very best acts, some even appeared on TV. Ed Sullivan's show on Sunday nights about 15 or 20 years ago was largely vaudeville. However some of the acts he used could not have showed in the early theaters; they took up too much space and used very large equipment. Sullivan paid his actors for one appearance, several times what they received when they were playing all over the country, showing at two different cities each week. I hope they all saved their money and are living in comfortable old age, since they gave us so much joy in their time.

The Lansing Theater Building at 13th and P in downtown Lincoln. It was later known as the Oliver, Liberty and finally the Varsity before being razed for the present National Bank of Commerce.

THE OLD ELLIOTT SCHOOL

They didn't have kindergarten in David City in 1906, so I started the first grade at age five. That year I came down with almost all of the children's diseases — this was usual in the days before inoculations. After whooping cough, I went on whooping for months and got very thin, so mother kept me out of school. I lost about a half a year.

We moved to Lincoln in June of 1907, and when I started to Elliott in September, mother decided I should repeat the first grade. I was lucky, as I drew a very fine teacher, Miss Merle Beattie, who later became director of elementary education for the city. The old Elliott was at 26th and O streets — a red brick building with a half basement which housed the lowest grades. Above were two more stories and an attic where we later took "domestic science." This building became a junior high school when the new Elliiott was built at 25th and N Streets.

The old Elliott's long wooden stairs were already beginning to be hollowed out by the many feet that trod them daily, and the school's playground was small. In my later years at Elliott the round slide fire-escape was installed — fire-alarms became very popular, and some children would come back after school to climb the slide and zip down again. I loved school and most of the teachers and graduated from Elliott's eighth grade in 1915.

Bleacher seats

The exercises were held in the old City Auditorium at 13th and M for all of the city's eighth grades. We sat in bleachers built on the stage. There were not enough tenors that year for the part-singing planned, so someone chose three girls from Elliott to sit with the boys and reinforce the tenor part. We didn't know whether to be happy or upset, and we did a lot of giggling at rehearsals. On graduation night, we sat there in our white dresses in a sea of dark suits, but we were not embarrassed enough to stop singing.

Miss Sadie Baird was Elliott's principal when we left and later went to the new Elliott, and was followed there by Miss Eunice Preston. My mother had made two apartments on the second floor of her home and Eunice was one of the tenants for many years.

In our last three years at Elliott we were "departmental" — an operating plan in which only one subject was taught in any one room and the students moved from room to room according to subject and time. It was the first step to the junior high school plan. This was good for me, as I was able to learn all the grammar I know from the diagrams on the blackboard in the English room. The curriculum was changing each year and grammar was never taught in the grade I was in.

We loved the orrery in the geography room and always begged to wind up the clockwork and watch the tiny brass planets and moons revolve around the bigger sun.

We liked one of the English teachers, Mrs. Grubb, very much, but we made fun of her clothes. Teachers all wore dark, plain dresses and we said Mrs. Grubb had bought a bolt of navy blue satin and made all her own things. They were much alike, with different collars and cuffs. I saw a good deal of her in later years, when she used to come to all my book-talks at the YWCA. Then she was always dressed in high style and seldom wore navy.

Life was hard for the left-handed in those days; both school and home tried to change them. The teacher put the pencil in the pupil's right hand and the paper at the "right" angle on the desk. Jeannette Farquhar, who won her battle as a determined "leftie," always wrote with her hand bent at an awkward angle above the paper.

Girls took sewing up in the attic during the sixth grade and each of us made a cap and apron to wear in cooking later. The large mop-cap covered all of the hair and half the face. The apron had a complete skirt all around long and full, with a large bib and shoulder straps which buttoned to the waist-band in back. We made those long french seams all by hand in the heavy white muslin. There were three buttonholes and mine were terrible. Mother had to buy larger buttons than those intended. I never wore this apron after cooking lessons; I wonder what happened to it.

Cooking instruction

I enjoyed cooking. Fannie Farmer had recently introduced standard measurements and I bothered my poor mother, trying to wean her away from her "little blue cup," her "butter the size of an egg" and a "heaping teaspoon." In class we were taught to make things in a double boiler in the old slow method and I insisted in doing this at home. Mother would say, "You'll never get a meal on the table when you have to cook for a family."

School was fun. Two living members of my class agree with most of my memories; we never seemed to have any official parties at school, but we had many private ones, inviting the same boys and girls. I was a very slow bloomer and now I can identify only one of the boys in the picture we found, and I knew him well in later years. In the eighth grade I did acquire a boy friend, Paul Yule, who was a head shorter than I. He walked me home from school and parties and put a candy bar on my desk every day after lunch. I was always slow getting back from the noon break and the bar appeared for almost two weeks before I sneaked in early one day and identified the donor. He was nice and I liked him very much, but I was very self-conscious about my height. (I was full grown at thirteen but most of the girls in my class added several inches in high school).

And now I am not sure which one he is in the picture.

For Teachers, Parents

I remember the fruit showers for the teacher when we were in the lower grades and plotting with another teacher to call ours out of the room so we could get the apples, etc. up on her desk. I remember the presents we always made for our parents. Penwipers were popular in those days before fountain pens. They were layers of felt, cut out and stitched together with covers we decorated. Calendars were supplied and we painted covers for them. Each class gave a formal program each year, when parents came and we "spoke pieces," sang and gave little plays.

I have only one sad memory of Elliott, and as always, it was nobody's fault but mine. After lunch on the last day, purple ribbons were awarded to those who had perfect attendance during the preceding year. They also went to an honor picnic at Capitol Beach. I was often late and with my chronic bronchitis and what I know now were allergies, I was often absent. But during this last year I had made a perfect record and came back to the last session—late!

This was the only time I ever wept at school.

The eighth grade graduating class at Elliott School in 1915. Gladys Schaaf is third from the left in the back row, Belle Farman is third from the right in the front row and Edith Hornby is directly in front of Gladys.

CLOTHED IN FORMALITY

Driving home from the Lincoln City Library one very warm February day this winter, I saw three girls, about 13, who were walking near a grocery store. School was just out and I wondered if they had worn those outfits to school or had changed in the restroom. For all three were barefoot and wearing bikini bathing suits. Though the temperature was in the 70s and I was comfortable in a light sweater, they looked chilly.

This set me to thinking of my childhood days, before World War I and the extreme formality of the clothes we wore. We changed to summer clothing by the calendar, not to celebrate a warm day in February. Men changed to straw hats about the middle of May, all of them at once, like the swallows returning from the south.

Still in wool

In February, we may have carried our heavy coats home from school, but we still were wearing woolen dresses, or middies with serge pleated skirts, long underwear, long stockings and high buttoned shoes. And if we had ever lost our minds and put on our bathing suits after school, we still would have been warm enough, because these suits had bloomers to the knees under a skirted dress and elbow sleeves. Plus long stockings and rubber slippers. How did we learn to swim?

Even if bikinis had been invented, nobody would have dared to appear in one. Someone would have called the police. Not even boys wore shorts. To school, they wore Norfolk jackets and knickers or a three-piece suit, with a white shirt and necktie. We all wore old clothes for play and girls were not allowed to wear trousers of any length. It would not have occurred to us to wear them, anyway.

Until 1910, ladies wore their skirts to the ground, changing to ankle length for tennis, ice-skating and golf. Men started wearing "plus-fours" about this time and many played tennis in white flannels.

48

When high-laced shoes out-moded the button-hook, a good many men and a few women wore spats over the laces. Many women wore slippers in the summer, usually white, changing about the time men went to straw hats. As women's figures always change with the new fashions, all ladies then tried to look like the Gibson Girl. She wore a pompadour, and had a buxom figure, with a high bosom (all in one piece) and a prominent fanny (but not a bustle). Men wore stiff, separate collars, attached by studs to the shirt. Nobody had ever heard of a soft-collared sport shirt or a dress shirt with an attached collar. At home a man might remove his collar in hot weather, but this was thought vulgar. My father never went without a collar at home, but he would take off his coat, vest and necktie. He always hung these in the breakfast room. If a lady came to the front door, father would run through the kitchen, put on the things hung up and then saunter into the parlor, "properly" dressed.

We wore our old clothes for leisure or work. Some men wore coveralls to work in the yard. But mother could never break my father of digging in his roses wearing his good suit. He was a very big man and had to have everything made for him by a tailor; and mother was very tight with the family money.

To work in the house, most women wore a cotton or light wool skirt, with a top called a "waist," not a shirt or blouse in those days. Over this one wore a voluminous apron and underneath, a shirt, corset, corset-cover and at least one petticoat.

To work around the house, most women wore their clothing a little looser fitting than their dress-up things. Quite a few older women, usually quite fat by the time they were in their fifties or sixties, took to wearing Mother Hubbard dresses at home. These were usually made of calico and were cut much like the Hawaiian muumuu dress, except that they always had long sleeves.

All females wore corsets after they were about thirteen, and almost all the other girls I knew wore them all through high school and college. When mother brought home a junior corset for me when I was in the eighth grade, I looked at this object with utter horror and refused to try it on. It was relatively shapeless (as we were at thirteen), and had bones around it and laced up the back, just like an adult corset. Where the adult affair had a sort of a lower half of a brassiere at the top, the girl's corset had an area of pleated silk, which would allow room for the growing breasts.

This contraption looked like an iron maiden to me and I refused even to try it on. Mother and I fought over it all winter and I finally won. I never wore a corset in my life. When all young women joined me in the late twenties, I started wearing the softer, more comfortable girdles.

All the girls I knew wore corsets. Many of them would even appear at gym class with the corset still on under the gym suit. The teachers did a good deal of checking and would often send a girl back to the dressing room to change. Most women even wore them under the skirted, bloomered, voluminous bathing suits of the period.

Since mother believed that going without a corset was very bad for the health besides being immoral in some way, she allowed me to wear the kimona dresses, which I discovered as I learned to sew after school was out. These dresses were related to the Mother Hubbards, but were shorter and had elbow sleeves cut in one with the body of the dress. They were easy to make and iron and they didn't touch my body anywhere, so Mother thought I looked decent wearing them. I made several at once and took them to camp when I went with five other girls that July.

Of course, I took the usual middies and pleated skirts that most girls wore those days, and wore them when our chaperone told me I must. I never looked at myself in the mirror, so I didn't know how dreadful I looked in the kimona dress; I was comfortable, and that is all I cared about in those days. I even climbed trees in them. (Of course, I wore the usual voluminous bloomers underneath.)

I still don't care what sort of clothes I wear, as long as I am decently covered and not too many years out of fashion. When slacks came into style, I began to wear them with great pleasure, not only for sports and in the garden, but everywhere. I still do. I own only three skirted outfits and I am sorry to see slacks becoming less popular. I will probably have to make them for myself eventually, but I still intend to wear them. They are very comfortable for an old lady.

Ankle erotic zone

Ladies did not have legs; in my childhood, they were supported by "lower limbs." It was a terrible shock if a summer breeze would lift the long skirt and show the ankle above a low slipper. The ankle was the only possible erotic zone and drew all male eyes, even when encased in a heavy dark stocking.

Necks were covered by a high collar of the dress material or by a boned, tight-fitting net collar coming right up to the ears. This was often attached to a net dickey which filled in the V-neck of a dress. Mother did not own an evening dress until late in the 1920s and this was not cut very low. But before the war, ladies of fashion wore very low cut formal evening dress and this was a shocking contrast to the daytime cover-up.

No "lady" ever left her own front door without wearing a hat, gloves and often carrying an umbrella or a parasol. Handbags were small and did not contain the large collection of miscellaneous junk which burdens mine today. A lady carried a handkerchief, a spare pair of gloves and a little small change. There was not any makeup, except perhaps a small booklet of powder leaves for her nose.

50

I never left the house without hearing my mother call, "Do you have a clean hanky, Gladys?" Kleenex, the blessing, appeared when I was teaching school in the 1920s. Because I had many colds, I had almost always packed a number of my father's large white linen handkerchiefs when I left home in September. So I suppose Father also was glad when we began to use Kleenex. It was my job at home to iron all the dozens of linen handkerchiefs for a large family and it seemed an unending job. Young women today should say a prayer of thanksgiving for Kleenex and wash and wear fabrics.

Before the war, hats were large cartwheels, called Merry Widows. These had very large crowns to fit over the enormous, elaborate coiffures. The pompadour was combed up over a "rat," made of light horsehair fabric. But many women used a rat made of hair combings. A hair receiver sat on every dressing table, a part of a hand-painted dresser set. This was a low bowl, with a hole in the center of the cover. When you had saved a bushel or so of combings, you could have a switch made of your own hair. Mother had a great deal of hair, but even so she sometimes wore a switch. Since she never wore a pompadour, she never used that horrid wad of combings for a "rat."

Hard to wash

All this hair was hard to wash and there were not many beauty shops in those days. Most people used a cake of Castile soap and a lemon or vinegar rinse. Shampoos were not given as often as today, usually for a party or some other special occasion. This is probably the reason that "finecombs" were popular and in frequent use. Also, this was the reason that many teachers were forced to send a child home, with a note asking his mother to wash his hair. In such cases, I believe kerosene also was applied. This never happened to us.

Mother had to give us quite frequent shampoos because we were all white-blond. But she still used the finecomb for any sign of dandruff. There was no stigma attached to its use. Can one even **find** a finecomb in stores today?

SEWING AND MENDING

"Use it up, wear it out;
Make it do or do without."

People lived by this old saying when I was a child. My mother almost never sat down without a needle in her hand. The mending basket was always full. Housewives then turned collars, tore worn sheets down the middle and sewed the good edges together, let down hems, made over the older children's garments for the younger ones — when clothing went to the rag bag it was really worn out. Who has a rag bag today? Who mends stockings? Who makes handkerchiefs with fine hemstitched hems? Some of this work was to make things last longer and some could be classed as *fine* sewing, which many women did for recreation. There was no radio or TV and movies had not become very good or popular.

Mother never learned to knit, so she did not put new heels in our stockings as many Europeans still do; but then we never wore those heavy woolen stockings. Ours were cotton, even in the winter, and Mother's mending was smooth to wear and beautiful to look at.

Little time to sit

Of course, women did not have much time to sit in those days, even if there were a hired girl. Housework took too much time; with few labor saving appliances and when foods were all cooked from "scratch." In the afternoon, if Mother had a free moment she sewed at the treadle machine in the good north light of the big dining room window. Here she did machine mending with great skill, lifting the pressure foot and sewing back and forth over a tear in a sheet or a pair of knickers. Also she put on many patches by machine. Everybody had patches on play clothes then, so we never felt embarrassed. I never became really expert at machine mending or patching, although I learned to darn stockings quite well. I remember how guilty I felt in the 1940s when, faced with an overflowing basket of worn socks, I threw them all away. I never turned a collar and never became really first-rate at embroidery. I did terrible satin stitch monograms on my best wedding-present sheets and never tried this stitch again. I made doilies and dresser scarves as presents for Mother — she continued to cover the tops of all furniture as long as she lived. I made her lunch cloths and napkins with very simple stamped embroidery. Mother did her own stamping. She could buy a paper pattern and then cut out the motif she needed. This was transferred to the cloth with a hot iron and there was her pattern, outlined in pale blue dots. I never even tried to learn the fine buttonhole scallops and cut-work that were her·specialty. I did learn hemstitching and also did a little drawn work.

Fine embroidery, like any other skill, takes constant and *intelligent* practice, and I wanted instant perfection. Although I could see what was wrong with the product of my efforts, I would not pick out the error and do the work over. Mother had several older sisters who did the housework and left her free to learn fine sewing, and then free to do it for the household. She often said that she did not know how to cook when she was married. I loved to cook and I got in her way in the kitchen, trying out some new concoctions which the family often did not like and refused to eat. But I was learning.

During the year Mother made some of our everyday clothing. We bought my father's suits and shirts, and heavy winter coats for everyone. However, twice a year — a few weeks before Easter and again shortly before school began in the fall — the seamstress would come for two weeks. We moved the bed out of the big north room upstairs and carried up the machine and a large table. Out went the carpet so it was easy to sweep up the threads and the scraps from the bare floor. The whole family got ready to fetch and carry for Mrs. Jewell, who lived with us for those two weeks and was just like one of the family. Her real skill was in designing and making better dresses (hers seldom looked "home-made"). At our house, though, she had to spend most of her time making nightshirts, underwear and children's garments. We wore our "best" dresses for school the next year and then for play if they were not outgrown.

Allowance for growth

Everything was made to allow for growth. Inside the deep hem of a dress was a big tuck (one to let down before the hem had to come out). Sometimes there was an inner tuck in the bodice just above the waist. All seam allowances were very wide so they could be let out if necessary.

Since she didn't have to make any sports clothes, Mrs. Jewell worked on our "best" dresses. She would cut out a dress, sew it together, and then Mother would join her upstairs to do the finishing by hand.

Curtains were also made at home. We did not have any draperies; there were just glass curtains, all alike, over the house. They were narrow panels of thin scrim or similar material, with a casing for the rod and a deep hem. These were simply shirred along the curtain rod and no hooks were used. When we first moved to 28th Street, Mother used lace curtains at the two big front windows (these came from David City). When they were discarded, Mother did not hang any more lace—she said it was too much work. When our window panels were washed, they were dried on the curtain stretcher in the back yard. I pricked fingers on those stretcher's sharp points many times.

As soon as Mother had sewed all the snaps or buttons on all our new clothes, she had to get back to her mending basket. We always used the dining room as a sitting room in the evenings. It was the largest room in the house, and the chandelier hung low over the table for studying and games. As soon as Irene and I were old enough, Mother would assign us to do the dishes after supper while she would settle down on an old sofa (so located on the west wall that she could keep an eye on us in the kitchen) and take a sock to mend. We had no table lamps in those days, but at her left stood the only floor lamp we owned; it had a large pink shade and long gold fringe. Father would sit, reading, in his big chair just beyond the lamp. Ade was supposed to be doing his homework at the table and we would join him, if we ever finished the dishes.

After supper company would often drop in. People seemed to visit around more then. Mother would stop mending socks and pick up the pretty velvet bag which held her finer sewing or embroidery. In the parlor, she would sit talking while she hemstitched a napkin or sewed pin-tucks for a "lingerie dress."

Lingerie party dress

These dresses were hold-overs from the nineteenth century. Worn as best party dresses for most girls through high school, they deserve mention. Put together almost entirely by hand, they were of lace insertion and narrow strips of fine white cotton material, almost always tucked. After a square of fabric was constructed the rough size of a sleeve, for instance, one cut out the sleeve from the pattern piece. In 1880, all seams were sewed by hand but by 1910, Mother would use a very fine needle and do the long skirt seams on the machine. For the waist of the dress, the lace always ran vertically, but several rows might run around the lower part of the skirt, above the hem.

Mother made my dress in 1913 and after it was let out, I wore it for my high school graduation. For that occasion, Mother had to add two more tucked strips to the front of the waist and several inches to the skirt. This was a lot of work, of course, but since the fabric was constructed in strips, the alterations did not show. Many families cherish heirloom baby dresses made this way all by hand. If they were made around 1901, when I was born, they have the very long skirt which spread out on the floor when baby sat on mother's lap.

The lingerie dress was worn only for very special occasions. As appropriate for the particular occasion one might wear a sash of different color. I used to save my money for a new sash quite often, because no one wanted to wear a big bow which had been tied too many times.

I never owned a hat to match my dress—they were expensive. They were made by hand over a wire frame. In the summer I always wore a big leghorn straw hat. Winter hats were usually made of thick satin, made over a heavy padded wire frame. There were a few felts, often thick fuzzy velour.

Irene never wanted to wear anything old or made over, so it was quite hard to persuade her to wear her lingerie dress when she graduated. They were going out of style by 1923 and many of her friends were going to have "boughten" dresses.

My younger sister, born in 1914, never had a lingerie party dress. By her time, all little girls wore the popular "pantie dress" until they were twelve or so. This garment had a short skirt. We had worn our skirts to mid-calf, even as small children. Magazine pictures of little French girls always made them look very odd to us, with their very short skirts. Under the dress, Marjorie wore matching panties, with a cuff below the knee, just like boy's knickers. At that age, we older girls had worn sateen bloomers, with elastic at the knee.

The plain straight "Dutch" bob came in about this time and Marjorie never had to undergo the torture of sleeping on curl rags and having snarls combed out of long hair.

Life was becoming a little easier for the housewife and sewing was much more simple. By the time the first World War was over, dresses had become a sort of sack, tied in the middle and with much less trimming. By the time I was married in 1929, we were buying most of our clothes. The few dresses we made could be "run up" in the afternoon and worn to a party that night. After only a few more years, everyone had an automatic washer—and by the 1940s many people had dryers. The world had changed and the housewife's work had really lessened at last.

RIDING THE TRAIN

Before the automobile age, you traveled by train—there was no other way to get there. Oh, you could drive the horses fifteen miles or so to shop in the nearest larger town. Or you could make a longer journey, very slowly, camping out overnight or staying with a farmer in settled country. Or, as did our pioneer ancestors, you could travel a very long distance with oxen and a covered wagon. But by 1910 the branch railroads had almost reached every small town, and it was widely accepted that the railway was the way to go.

In 1907, Mother took the three of us children to visit her parents, who had moved from Omaha to Barnesville, Minnesota soon after Mother was married. She took us out of school early (this was the year we moved to Lincoln in the summer) and we were gone for five or six weeks. You didn't visit for just two or three days then. We boarded the train at David City one morning, changed in Lincoln for Omaha, and waited a few hours there to catch a "sleeper" to Minneapolis. There we stayed a few days with my Aunt Kate and then took another train to Barnesville in western Minnesota. That was the only time I ever saw my McDunn grandparents. They were nearly seventy then. My mother was to go alone to Grandma's funeral six or eight years later.

1907 Trip

On this 1907 trip we youngsters were six, four and two, respectively. I asked Mother once how she managed such a trip with three little children. She replied, "Oh, it wasn't bad. You were pretty children and behaved well. Someone was always asking to play with the baby (Irene). At stations, some man would always offer to carry her and someone else would carry the bags." Also, there were plenty of redcaps at large stations in those days and they would carry your bags for 10¢ each.

Mother had checked two big trunks through to Barnesville, but she needed lots of clothes for the trip and the short stay with Aunt Kate, so she also carried two big bags. When we left David City we also brought a lunch in a shoebox. Mother also had a small, wicker basket filled with items needed on the train; such as a washcloth and soap and a small, collapsible silver cup. There were no paper cups or drinking fountains on trains yet; just a tap with a tin cup on a chain. Mother didn't need to bring diapers as Irene was reliably "trained" at two-and-one-half. We visited around . . . Grand-pa's, Uncle Ed's and Uncle Tom's. Each had several children and we had a very good time. We were used to farms.

Every summer, nearly always over the Fourth of July when Dad could join us, we went to the old farm near Woodbine, Iowa. Mother's very much older brother Frank had taken over the farm years before, when the younger family had moved to Omaha—Mother was ten at that time. These trips were not vacations for Mother, as Uncle Frank was a widower with two half-grown children who were supposed to keep house, but didn't do it very well. Mother cooked, cleaned, and canned. And one year, when the harvest was early, she cooked for threshers. Here she had assistance, as old friends living in the neighborhood came to help with the seemingly endless cooking.

We still went to Woodbine each summer after we had moved to Lincoln, and I was old enough to remember one July Fourth when Ade let a firecracker blow up in his hand. I can still see the small buggy dashing up the road to town taking him to the doctor. He did not lose any fingers, and recovered from the cuts and lacerations.

Uncle Frank married again about 1910 and we gradually ceased going there as Mother did not care for his new wife, and was no longer needed to do the work. Not long after this, we started camping at Crete.

We also made one or two trips to visit my father's sister Mary, who lived on a farm near Beattie, Kansas. Our Iowa relatives never visited us, not even once, but Aunt Mary came to Lincoln each year, with all her children.

Shoebox lunch

We loved the trains! We loved eating lunch from the shoebox. It was always the same—fried chicken, deviled eggs, fruit, cookies, and bread and butter sandwiches, sometimes a few with ham or cheese fillings. We didn't have a Thermos bottle in those days (perhaps they had not yet been invented). We drank the water from the tap at one end of the car, taking turns with mother's little silver cup. Mother could buy a cup of coffee from the train "butcher." This was a boy who came through the car every half hour or so with tin cups and a big tank of coffee already sugared and creamed, but never strong and never hot—on his back. He also made other trips carrying snacks and selling cheap books and small gift items. He was part of the enter-tainment that kept the kids busy on long trips.

There were other delights on a train. If the conductor was not too high and mighty, we would talk to him. We would listen to the conductor or the brakeman call the name of the next stop, and since we were usually on a local train, there were many stops. Mother could sometimes understand the calls but we never could. We also talked to (or should I say bothered?) other passengers, who were usually very nice about it. Mother had picture books in her basket, and once in a while we could be induced to sit still for a few minutes. We behaved much like small children on a long automobile trip today, except that we were free to run up and down the aisle.

Unless we were in a Pullman Mother would have someone help her turn one seat over, thus giving us a little area of our own. Ade and I would take turns resting in the second seat, or perhaps we were small enough for both to use it at the same time. Irene slept most of the time, since she was so young.

Although most of our train trips were fairly short, we were usually drooping with weariness when we arrived at our destination. Still, we loved it!

Solo journey

My first trip alone was in the summer of 1919 after I had graduated from high school. I took the Rock Island during the night to Geneseo, Illinois. A teacher friend of Mother's, home there for summer vacation, had invited me to spend July with her. I can't imagine why, unless she thought she was doing Mother a favor by taking an eighteen-year-old girl off her hands for a month. I don't think I could have been a very desirable guest. Her friends were all much older, and although they were lovely to me and invited me to lunch and introduced me to their daughters and young friends, I was not very interested in them. I was *really* only interested in boys at this point and I had left my heart in Lincoln and wasn't nice to the occasional boy Jessie rounded up for me. Perhaps the Lincoln boy was the reason I was allowed to — or sent — to visit the Illinois friend.

All the same, I enjoyed the trip on the Pullman. I wanted to have breakfast on the train. Unfortunately, I had to get off at Geneseo so early in the morning that I didn't have time to eat much after the dining car opened. I did better on my next trip, though. In late September I traveled to Terre Haute, Indiana for my year at Saint Mary's College. On this trip I had plenty of time for breakfast before we got to Chicago, and I expect I established a record for the amount I ate.

Once in Chicago I had several hours to kill, so after a station "hack" took me across town to the Illinois Central Station, I took a streetcar downtown. Here I visited the Art Institute and had lunch. I think I also saw Marshall Field's store, but that may have been another trip. I talked to everybody, paying no attention to the warnings from home, and I survived. I judged all my later train rides from the one I enjoyed out of Chicago on the Illinois Central that evening. The linen was never so white and crisp;

the smiling waiters never so deft; the flowers on the tables never so lovely; nor the food never so good. This time, too, I ate both dinner and breakfast.

Yes, I loved riding on the railroad. However, after I was married and the roads and automobiles got better, and there began to be nice motels along the highways, my husband and I made our few long trips by car. Nearly everyone else was doing the same, so the railroads began to cut their passenger services. First they took the dining cars off the trains and people had to eat at snack bars or cars equipped with early vending machines. Next to go was Pullman service. "Roomettes" were invented instead; they required fewer porters.

Finally there were very few passenger trains left and the service became so bad that many travelers began to fly. They soon found, though, that much of the time flying saved en route was taken up by waiting in airports and driving between big cities and their airports.

More recent rides

There were still a few good trains left in the 1950s and 1960s. I would like to mention two trips I took in those decades.

In March of 1957 my husband and I took the California Zephyr and its Vistadome cars from Lincoln to San Francisco. We enjoyed the glassed domes and there was on that train operated by the Burlington, Rio Grande and Western Pacific railroads a real dining car. West of Denver the diner menu included trout, fresh from some mountain stream, and the tables were decorated with Colorado carnations. A stewardess took reservations for one of the dinner sittings, so there was no standing in line.

After the train arrived in Oakland, we were ferried across the bay (instead of going by bus) to San Francisco. The next day when we were to travel down to Lancaster, California, where our son lived, it turned out that a mistake had been made in our reservations, so we were given a bedroom at the front of the parlour car. After seeing the city on the bay for a day and a night, we boarded the Southern Pacific for our first deluxe trip. And we enjoyed it very much.

In 1960, going to New York, I rode on the Twentieth Century Limited, one of the really great luxury trains. We had roomettes, but they were across the aisle from each other, and with both doors open, the arrangement was almost as good as a bedroom compartment. In the dining room, each lady had a little pink orchid beside her plate, and a dewy white rose the next morning at breakfast. The food was not as good as that on my 1919 trip on the Illinois Central had been and it was much more expensive. Then again, so was everything else much more expensive in this later year.

I had a great disappointment on the 1960 trip. I asked the porter to call me early so I could sit at breakfast and look out of the big dining car windows as we traveled alongside the Hudson River toward New York City.

He did, and I did, only to stare out at a thick, blinding fog. I could not see West Point on the river's opposite bank, nor the New Jersey Palisades when we passed them. Worst of all, I could not see anything of the Washington Irving country, as I had planned.

I would like to take the Amtrak the next time I go to my son's place — he now lives in Pacific Palisades, California — for Christmas. Yet I hate to ask him to go to the Los Angeles Union Station to meet me, when it is so easy for him to go to the big airport from their house.

I still like trains the best!

The Burlington Railroad depot, looking north from the old overpass.

CAMPING OUT

Before the First War, there were very few organized camps for children near Lincoln, I knew of only the YMCA Camp Strader on the Big Blue River, near Crete. My brother went there several summers.

Most camping families rented a cabin in a large camp and took the whole group for a month or for all summer. Many camped in a rented tent at Epworth Park during the Chautauqua. We drove out every evening to see the show in the big tent but never camped there.

Many Lincoln families owned cabins at Lake Pelican, Minnesota, or Estes Park, Colorado. After school let out, they packed their trunks and traveled by train to camp. Papa would come out on several weekends and would help them come home over Labor Day weekend.

The Millers, who lived on our block, went to Estes in the middle of August, as Mr. Miller was a victim of severe hay fever. I think they stayed there until the first frost had killed the weeds, which meant their children missed some weeks of school.

Traveling, tenting

We knew only one family who traveled by car, camping in a tent each night along the way. They went to Seattle in 1917, over primitive roads, fording some streams or going miles out of their way to find a bridge, breaking down often and repairing a punctured tired every 30 miles or so; an epic adventure. One of the old car books shows such a group, with their car festooned with tent and baggage — there were no car trunks in the early days and fabric car tops had no luggage racks.

Most camping groups wore the khaki suits favored by famous explorers, taking only a few changes of underwear. Among those living in our neighborhood was Judge Cornish's family. Mrs. Cornish did not like to wash clothes while camping. She saved up all their old garments, and they wore them camping and threw them away when dirty.

Our family camped several summers at Horky's Park, upstream from Camp Strader, on the Big Blue. All but Father. He said he had seen enough of country living and considered tent or cabin camping nothing but dreadful. He stayed in Lincoln and ate in restaurants while we were gone. At least this made things a little easier for Mother, as we kids would eat anything and Father was fussy. I suppose she took us camping for our pleasure — it certainly was not a vacation for her.

We went the first time in 1912 for a month. Mother and the girls took the train. Father drove down with Ade and the luggage with old Fanny and the surrey. That was a long day. Horky's supplied canvas cots, a kerosene stove, a rough cupboard, a table and chairs, a few kettles, tin cups, dishes and very little else. I think we had kerosene lamps.

For several summers, we stayed in a large tent with high sidewalls and a large screened porch erected over a two-by-four frame on a wooden platform. As tents go, it was very good. The ice-box was half a barrel, sunk in the ground and covered with a wooden lid and wet burlap. A wagon brought out supplies from town and the ice came from the camp icehouse, cut from the river in the winter and stored in sawdust.

Chaperones

Mother did the washing on a board in a tub out in the yard, carrying water from the pump and heating it in the tent on the two-hole stove. Poor woman. We all got wet and dirty.

The next summer, 1913, we traveled to camp in our new car, the big red Velie. It had so little storage space that we couldn't pack everything in with the family, so Father had to make a second trip with the bedding, dishes, etc. In 1914, my intrepid mother took us again, with a new baby sister. This time she hired someone to do the washing, but she still had to work much too hard. We children had a wonderful time. We were 13, 11 and 9.

In 1915 Mother was very ill and we didn't camp as a family, but I went to Horky's for 10 days with five other girls, two mothers (as chaperones and cooks). We stayed in a cabin and it cost us $10 each. Toward the end of the week, Mrs. Wood said to us, "Girls, we have some money left. If you will live on creamed dried beef for the rest of the time, we can stay two more days." We did.

Many high school and college groups used to camp like this at Crete, taking a mother or older married sister as chaperone. The boys needed none, but sometimes brought a mother or older sister for a cook.

War ends all

The river was dangerously high during our stay in 1915 and we didn't spend much time in the water. It didn't matter much, since I didn't know how to swim. We went to Lincoln High School that fall and learned to swim when the pool opened second semester.

The war and Mother's ill health kept us from going to Horky's again. There was no interesting scenery there, no sparkling lake, no mountains. As an adult, I have camped in many more beautiful places, but nothing had ever equaled my memories of camping as a child, in a tent at Horky's Park and dipping all day in the murky Big Blue River.

There were few places to swim in Lincoln then and only Ade knew how. Mother made my swim suit, only I just paddled wearing it. It was of a stiff navy blue material (alpaca?) trimmed with yards of white braid. There was a sailor dress top to the knee and full bloomers below. With this, I wore long stockings and rubber swim slippers. No wonder I never learned to swim at Crete!

When Mother took us to Horky's again in 1916, I had the best time yet. The launch "Elaine" would take us upriver to a good sand bar and we went twice a day. We had taken my friend Fern with us and we were now old enough to attend the evening social meetings at the camp's central pavilion. I met a boy from Hastings, who liked me better than Fern. This was most unusual. We all went home and he didn't write to me as promised. (Girls did not write first in those days.) I was heartbroken, of course, and I never saw him again.

Boating on the Blue River near Crete.

63

DOLLAR DAY AT FAIR

"What day are you going to the FAIR?" we said. It was very different in my childhood and yet it was much the same. We went to Capitol Beach almost every Sunday and were given ten cents to spend.

But at the FAIR, they gave us a whole **dollar**. The rides cost more, but you could still get an ice cream cone or a big paper cone of cotton candy for a nickel. There were not as many rides and I was afraid to go on the huge Ferris wheel. The prizes at the shooting galleries and the various baseball throws were heavy on Kewpie dolls and almost never had anything that I wanted. Irene usually spent all her money by noon — I sometimes had a few cents left when we went home.

We drove out with old Fanny and the surrey, most years. Where did we leave her for the day? I hope there was a shed in the shade. We were always going back to the buggy for something. Mother almost always packed a big basket of food and we were always eating a piece of fried chicken or cake, in spite of the coins in our pockets. We usually ate our noon dinner at the Grace Methodist dining hall, famous for both quality and quantity of food. Although I was a "good eater," I could never manage to finish the first helping.

We arrived as soon as the gates were open and Father took us to see the chickens and the pigs the first thing. He had raised "fancy" chickens in David City, and I suppose he showed them at the Butler County Fair. Now he would borrow a long stick from some exhibitor and show us the fine points of the Bantams and some sort of red chickens with very long tails. We spent a lot of time with the pigs, also, which were enormously fat in those days, when people used a great deal of lard. We loved the baby pigs.

I liked to look at the fish, in the old building, over west of the present one. Mother took us to the other exhibits. We liked the fine arts, the various types of handicraft shown and especially the food.

There was no 4-H then, but a few girls showed embroidery, cake and cookies. I never thought of entering any of my work out there, but I would criticise freely. "Look, Mother," I would say, "That doily is not a bit better than the one I made you for your birthday," etc. But when next summer arrived, I did not think of sorting out my year's work and taking the best to the Fair.

There was very little knitting shown then, but a great deal of crochet and tatting. An early premium list has a class for handmade lace, three kinds, and many classes of more difficult sorts of embroidery. There was a class for senior citizens (over 60 then) baldly called "Old Ladies' Class." No euphemisms.

On one wall of the Agriculture Hall was a huge mural made of various colored apples and there was a life-size cow, sculptured of butter. One year they showed a large "Spirit of '76" in butter. It was always very hot at the Fair and no air conditioning. Why didn't the butter melt?

I remember the cakes as very tall, with an inch of frosting on top. The cookies were mostly rolled and cut out, or "rocks," dropped cookies. Women had just started making brownies and other cut cookies of this type.

We went to the races in the afternoon. The grandstand was made of wood, with enormous beams and braces overhead. The horses were trotters and the races were called harness or sulky races. The driver sat in a tiny, fragile looking little cart called a sulky. Mother wouldn't let my father bet, but he kept a record of his choices in a little book and of any wins he might have had.

After airplanes became common, there were flying shows over the center of the track. We saw men walking on the wings of those tiny biplanes and some stunting at very low altitudes. In 1919 a Lt. Locklear showed his famous trick of changing planes in mid-air.

In 1915, auto race driver Barney Oldfield gave exhibitions, but no records were made on the muddy track. He drove a big "French Flyer." Some of the important evening entertainments (such as a circus one year) were shown in front of the grandstand. As we grew old enough to stay at the Fair after supper, we also got to see the fireworks, which often finished off the day.

Mother wouldn't let us go into the sideshows, but we walked around looking at the huge posters and listening to the barkers out in front. Sometimes the fat lady would sit in front for a while and always the dancing girls showed themselves, wearing a great many clothes. Most years, there were letters to the paper, complaining about the immorality of the carnival.

These days, I enter some of my knitting at both the County and State Fairs, but I am no longer able to visit all the exhibits. I inspect one building and then go home. I watch the people more than the exhibits. But it is still the FAIR.

HALLOWEEN — FOR BIG BOYS

There was some confusion over the date of Halloween, back when I was a child.

Some of the "witches" roamed the neighborhood on the night of Oct. 30, while others did their damage the next night. Everyone has now settled on Oct. 31, All Hallow's Eve, the night before All Saint's Day (Nov. 1). But in the early days, people had to get ready for the 30th. Everything loose around the place must be padlocked in the barn or taken down to the basement, or the "witches" would move things to your neighbor's porch or down to the streetcar tracks on O Street.

My mother also saw that the screens were off and the storm windows put up. She said it was harder to get the soap off the screens than to wash it off the glass.

That was the only Halloween mischief that I ever got into, soaping windows. The only thing I could draw well was an Indian head with a big war bonnet of feathers, and I left my signature around the block, for anyone to see. Usually, I was safely inside at home, or escorted by Dad to a Halloween party.

This was a holiday that was celebrated mostly by big boys.

Extraordinary

Too bad the energy expended each year by the boys was never harnessed for useful purposes. Besides mixing up all the movable property to be found, they moved things not ordinarily disturbed.

The police were very busy these two nights, but I never heard that any boy was arrested. The damage was seldom as bad as the vandalism we read about today, not always on Halloween now, either.

I always wondered how the boys did it. Almost every year, someone's buggy was found on a church steeple or roof the next morning.

A friend told me that in his southeastern Nebraska town, the boys unloaded a wagon full of oats (from the elevator driveway), hoisted the wagon to the roof of a nearby shed, where it was found, again full of oats next morning. My friend was not along another year, when boys from miles around removed every privy in Brownville and set all of them up along the main street.

There were not many backyard toilets in Lincoln by the time we moved here, but there were some — two in our block. These were knocked over each year.

Many backyards had small coal sheds or other little shacks, easily pushed over and they always were.

Nowadays, we answer the doorbell to look down at a little "spook" in costume, clutching a big sack and piping "tricks or treats," while Mother or Dad lurks in the background. Before the war, the doorbell might ring, but you opened it to find a sack lying on your porch, **not** full of candy, and you heard the sounds of the big boys running away.

Selective action

In our block the damage was usually selective. We had two neighbor women who were hard on children the year around, and the youngsters might get back at these tormenters on this one night.

One of these women would not allow even the smallest children to skate on her driveway. The walks were more often brick in those days than smooth concrete and driveways were a popular skating rink. If a child even stopped on her front walk with muddy feet, this woman would dash out and scold, and then get the hose and wash the walk.

Another woman, who lived on a corner, carried on a perpetual feud with the kids who cut across her corner.

And neither of these old girls would tolerate a child in her backyard, for any reason.

Mrs. C, next door, always found her porch swing on a house porch three or four blocks down the street. Any front porch chairs left out would be left on another porch, or in another front yard. We never had any lawn furniture in those days, but we put away the hose and any yard tools not already in the barn for the winter.

We girls and smaller boys usually donned a costume and went to one of the many parties given in the neighborhood, where we "bobbed" for apples in a big tub and told ghost stories. In good weather there was often a backyard party, where we roasted wieners and marshmallows over a bonfire and sat around the dying fire to tell our stories. Hay rides, also, were popular for Halloween.

When "trick or treating" visiting began to replace the garbage bag boys on your front porch, some children overdid this. One house on Sheridan

Boulevard (a street that began to be built up during the first World War) was rumored to dispense big Hershey bars, then ten cents each. Each Holloween, cars from all over town, some filled with boys old enough to drive, converged at this block on Sheridan and it was said that many of these were from small towns around Lincoln.

When we lived on J Street, before 1970, we would see 20 or 30 groups of children at our door, with a few big boys among them. Now, although there are several small children in my neighborhood, I see very few on Halloween night. I prepare for them, leave on the porch light and stay home. Last year not one child rang my bell. Later, I had to give away my stock of candy, as I should not eat any. I miss the little "spooks," they were always so sweet.

But it never occurs to me to put away any hose still left out, and I almost never have my storm windows (combination) pushed down by Oct. 31. And I haven't had a window soaped since the 1930s when we lived in a small town.

OMAHA'S EASTER TORNADO

They were cyclones when I was a child; nobody called them tornadoes in those days.

We learned to name these storms properly after March 23, 1913. That was the day a tornado went east of Lincoln but came down to hit Omaha. Since it was Easter, there were not as many deaths as might have been expected with all the damage done, because schools and most businesses were closed.

Birthday

This date is very clear in my mind, because it was the first time in my 12 years that my birthday, March 25, had been after Easter and not in Lent. We stopped making fudge in the evenings and I usually gave up candy. March 23 was my friend F's birthday. All this makes the date and happenings very vivid in my memory.

Fright

We could never forget that Easter tornado, when we had the greatest fright of our lives. We did not get the Velie, our first automobile, until that summer, and our parents had taken Fanny and the surrey out to call on some friends who lived just south of the penitentiary. We were 12, 10 and 8 and old enough to be left alone in the afternoon. The sky grew very dark and the wind began to howl. We put on wraps and went out on the porch to watch the sky. The clouds were a horrible grey-green-yellow color and hung very low. We clung together and wished the folks would get home.

It got even darker and the wind blew harder; the big elms along our street were whipping around like saplings. It began to rain and we moved back close to the door. My sister was crying and I was trying not to weep, when we heard a running horse coming from the south on 28th Street.

Over the hill came the surrey, with Mother holding on and Father standing up and **whipping** poor old Fanny. (I don't think the whip had ever been out of the socket before.) He had trouble slowing the horse for the turn into our steep driveway. They put Fanny into the barn, still wearing her harness and they got very wet. They hurried us under the back stairs, where we crouched for some time.

After the rain stopped, we unharnessed the horse and put the buggy away, all of us helping and keeping together. Then we went back into the house and Mother made cocoa before she changed her wet clothes. (Cocoa was the universal panacea). Everything outdoors was covered with a yellow mud from that strange rain, but it was getting lighter and the wind had gone down a little. Before long we heard the paperboys shouting "Extra!" coming out on O Street and we read about Omaha and the great tornado that had missed us.

'Cyclone cellar'

There had been a large "cyclone cellar" in the side yard of our David City house and Mother used it for a root cellar to store the sacks of potatoes and other "keeping" vegetables. The depth must have been well below the frost line, so it was warm in winter and cool in summer. We never had to use this cave to shelter from a tornado, but it was in constant use for storage. We always called it just "the cave." There were shelves built at the far end and Mother kept some of her canned vegetables and jams down there because our house did not have a basement. Most farms and many houses in Nebraska then had caves, and many families were saved by their depth when they lost house, barn and all their stock in a tornado.

The Omaha tornado made a very deep impression on us and the next summer, 1914, my brother and I, with the help of three neighbor boys who were 11 and 12, dug a good-sized cave in our big back yard. We worked on it all during vacation and moved a huge pile of heavy yellow clay. That was the year my youngest sister was born in February and so my father had to help us. He got some heavy beams and thinner sheathing boards to lay across the top and he helped us put these in place and cover them with tar-paper. Then came the really hard work because we had lost interest; school had begun and we had to be forced to put all that dirt back on top.

It was worse than practicing the piano.

Then, just before cold weather, we made steps at one end, using half railroad ties, and Father made a frame and a door over them, taking off the door to an unused closet in the furnace room.

I was 14 the next summer and had stopped playing with the boys much, but they used it for several more years and even built a working fireplace at the far end. The boys plotted to "get" me one day when they were mad at me. (Was I asking to play with them at my advanced age?) They asked me to show them how to brown the meat for a stew — then they all ran out and sat on the slanting door, after covering the chimney with a flat rock. I put out the small fire with the water in their bucket and sat down there in the dark, fuming and getting soaked in smoke, until they got tired and went away. I'm certain that it was the very last time I played with the boys (until they wanted me to teach them how to dance in a few more years).

A typical scene of the Easter tornado's devastation.

71

HIGH SCHOOL DAYS

It was June 1915 when I graduated from the eighth grade at the old Elliott School at 26th and O streets. One of the biggest joys was knowing that Lincoln's beautiful new high school at 22nd and J would be ready for us in September. We often drove by the new building during the summer just to look at it; it was "the finest new school in the country," the newspaper said. The outside looked finished but the grounds were bare and unplanted. Lincoln had needed a new upper school for many years. The old one, plus the McKinley grade school and the Board of Education Administration building, had been there too many years, crowded together on the block (bounded by M, N, 15th and 16th streets) where Pershing Municipal Auditorium stands today.

The old high school was crowded and noisy, and the grounds were too small for physical education to be held near the school. The buildings were wearing out and the heating plant broke down more than once. In 1910 ink froze in classroom inkwells and in 1911 some steam pipes exploded. Later that year, Lincoln voters approved a bond issue to pay for a new high school.

Many citizens wanted to build two new high schools then — one north and one south. Others wanted to rebuild on the old downtown site. There were continual arguments about just where to build a single school. Even after the bond issue passed, two suits were filed against the new plans, one after the construction contract had been signed. The Supreme Court decided both cases in favor of building the new school and of the site at 22nd and J. The cornerstone was laid on June 20, 1913.

The beautiful new building, with marble walls and stairways, terrazzo floors and good lighting from numerous windows and from the inside courts, originally cost $750,000. Some say it could not be duplicated today for $25 million.

When we entered in September 1915 we were the first class to spend all four of our high school years in the new building. We were a lively and talented class with both good and bad records. We were almost not allowed to graduate because of an incident with the Junior Class boys during our class picnic. Our Senior Class Day and the Junior-Senior Dance were cancelled. (I don't remember that the juniors were punished at all — surely it was not punishment when the authorities cancelled the dance the juniors were supposed to give us). Our class was so hurt that we did not give the usual present to the school when we left. We gave that money to the French war orphans or the Red Cross. Some years later, as alumni, we gave some money to the high school library.

Alumni reunions

As Lincoln High School alumni, we met two or three times in our college years, and then waited until our fiftieth anniversary to have another reunion. I was on the committee which worked on the plans for nearly two years. The co-chairmen, the late Clarice and Clifford Hicks, usually held the meetings at their house. It was a good committee. The late Arnott Folsom gave us some money for postage at our first meeting and quite a few alumni sent a few dollars in their answers to our first letter. My job was to draft the letters; one of the men had these typed and duplicated in his office.

We had another smaller reunion for our fifty-fifth in 1974 and a third with less than thirty people in 1979. Those of us who are left will probably not get together again.

The LHS classrooms were ready for us in that September of 1915 but there was still much work left to be done on the building. You could easily stumble over a bucket of plaster in the hall and the lockers were not in place for two or three weeks. I had registered for physical education and found that the gymnasiums and the locker rooms were ready, but not the swimming pool.

Scarcely any girls knew how to swim then, so most of us took swimming as soon as the pool was ready. When the swim suits were issued on the first day, we were shocked. We had never seen any swimwear for women except the voluminous skirted suits with bloomers to the knee. These new "Annettte Kellermans" were tight and made of thin grey cotton. If their design had resembled a modern swimsuit, we probably would have refused to wear them. But they were cut high in the back and front and the legs came half-way to the knees. But there was *no skirt* and we felt naked in them. After a few weeks, we got used to the suits and wore them at exhibitions and intramural swim meets (the only kind we ever had). We were not taught what was then called the Australian crawl — we learned only the old breast stroke with the frog kick and the side and back strokes. I could float well, learned to swim quickly and enjoyed it very much. The events in our little swim meets were very different from those today.

Swimming events

The Advocate (the Lincoln High school newspaper) of November 17, 1917 lists the following events at a swim meet for our boys team in Omaha:
1. Underwater swim (no length given).
2. Plunge for distance.
3. One length swim (no distance or stroke given).
4. Two length swim (no distance or stroke given).
5. Fancy diving.
6. Relay (no distance or stroke given).

I was only just good enough to make the freshman girls basketball team. We didn't do very well, but the next year as sophomores we won the round-robin tournament. Our class also won as seniors, but I didn't practice enough to get on that team. I did keep up my memberships in the Mummers (drama club) and Writers Club.

Those two clubs had not even organized in 1915. There were still sororities and fraternities in high school then. The boys' groups had Greek names and were not officially connected with the school. The girls' societies used such names as Shakespeare Club and were organized as literary societies. Their meetings were reported in the school paper and they had faculty sponsors, but they were sororities, just the same. They gave rush parties and pledged their new members. I had never heard of them until my friend Fern Jackson was asked to join one of them. Since her mother did not believe in closed clubs in high school, Fern was not allowed to join. I was happy enough, going around in a busy dream and taking part in the activities which interested me. I had "killed" my chances in one club in the first few weeks of school, by sitting, uninvited, at "their" table in the cafeteria.

The Advocate of October 24, 1917, had an article about literary societies in high school. There had been a survey of their effect in a number of schools and Lincoln High came out with a very low grade, so there were to be a lot of new rules. No more rushing—the clubs were to meet the girls at school; there could be no more parties held away from school and there were a lot of new restrictions on hours, etc. Groups could not hold down a club table in the cafeteria. I don't know if the clubs just died out after the new rules or whether the school authorities suppressed them as they did the boys' groups about the same time. Of course there had always been a few open clubs which any girl could join if she wished, such as the Girl's Club, which was sponsored by the YWCA. Others, such as the Chemistry Club, could be joined if you were taking the course.

To enter Writers Club, I submitted a terribly sad story about the Prince of Wales (who became England's King Edward VIII, later abdicated and died as the Duke of Windsor). When this effort was read aloud at a later club meeting, I was very much ashamed of it. I was a typical adolescent, shy one moment and over-bold the next. I turned out to be a good actress because I could lose myself in the character I was playing. Mummers Club was formed in 1917. When I tried out for this new club, I wrote and acted in a little playlet with two other girls.

Writer and actress

I took the college preparatory course which had so many requirements that there wasn't much room for electives. I am especially glad that I took typing somewhere in there. I have forgotten all my shorthand but the typing has been very useful over all these years. Courses in French and Spanish were not yet offered when I was in high school. I took German my first year, because my father wanted me to, but switched to Latin for the next six semesters. I was lucky enough to draw Miss Jessie Jury for Latin. One of the great teachers in my life, she was a tiny little woman who maintained perfect order in her classroom. Despite her diminutive stature, she had an air of authority that dominated students.

My home room teacher, Miss Margaret Proctor, taught me math for four years. She was also stern in the classroom, but I soon learned to love her. It was very hard to flunk any of her courses. She kept you after school every day, if necessary, and she stayed with you till six o'clock if she had to. After she retired from teaching, she used to come to my book talks at the YWCA, sitting in the front row and beaming at me. She was still correcting my pronunciation after many years. She became a very good friend whom I miss greatly now that she is gone.

I took eight straight semesters of English. We read one novel and one Shakespeare play in *every* semester. This does *not* include book reports. The novels were *Silas Marner, A Tale of Two Cities, Oliver Twist, The Scarlet Letter, Les Miserables, Huckleberry Finn, The Last of the Mohicans* and another which has escaped my memory. Along with all this reading we did a good deal of theme writing and had to memorize twenty lines or so from every play. In later years when I was pulling a trailer, I used to while away the long dull stretches of road by shouting Shakespeare into the desert wind. I am thankful that we were not required to memorize anything from George Eliot. Besides being my outstanding English teacher, Miss Sarah T. Muir was a very interesting woman outside of school. The Advocate of October 3, 1917 reported that she had spent her summer vacation in New York City helping the workers for Women's Suffrage.

Until I took Medieval History at the University of Nebraska, the "Dark Ages" were indeed dark to me. In high school, Ancient History ended with the decline of Rome and skipped at once to American History, which we studied very thoroughly for three more years.

I was too tall for many parts in plays. In our junior play, I had a very small speaking part which I learned in a few days, after learning and practicing the female lead all through weeks of practice. The coach told me finally that although I was very good, I just didn't *look* the part. The 1918 picture of the cast shows me looking down in the mouth and I remember that I thought life wasn't worth living.

I wasn't too tall for the role of Lady Brachnell in "The Importance of Being Earnest," our senior play, and it was a good part. We borrowed my costume from Miller & Paine's better suit department. It was a very expensive garment for those days. The price was over $200 and the hat was $25.

I served on the Advocate staff for one semester in my junior year and took journalism for my English course the semester before (that is why I remember only seven novels read in class). I was always busy writing something and had two short pieces in the 1918 and 1919 edition of the Links, the Lincoln High yearbook.

My high school days were lively and interesting and very different from today's school. We didn't wear caps and gowns but went to our baccalaureate services on a middle June Sunday wearing dark suits and colored summer dresses. For graduation the next evening at St. Paul's Methodist Church downtown, the girls wore their white party dresses. We were now officially grown up and most of us never wore those dresses again.

Lincoln High School as it was nearing completion in 1914.

WYXTRA! THE WORLD AT WAR

My children heard about Pearl Harbor on the radio. But we learned of the first World War through the **extra paper**. These extras were great events in my childhood. I remember those for the sinking of the Titanic and the start of the European war and the one telling us that the United States had declared war on Germany on April 6, 1917.

The paper boys would come running out from town on O Street, shouting "WYXTRA! WYXTRA PAAAAPA- READ ALL ABOUT IT!" My father would get up and pull on his trousers over his night-shirt and hurry to the corner of 28th and O streets to buy a paper. We all got up and he would read us the big news. Then mother made cocoa and we went back to bed.

The war did not make much difference in our lives until the United States got in. American industry, especially ship-building, had a big boost. After Germany stepped up its submarine warfare and hit our shipping badly, and especially after the Lusitania was sunk, we began to pay more attention.

German class

When I started high school in 1915, a member of the first freshman class in the new Lincoln High School at 22nd and J, I took German. Because my father spoke German as a first language and did not learn much English until he went to school, we thought he remembered enough to help me with my pronunciation. But the anti-German sentiment was growing rapidly in the middle west and the classes in German were thrown out in the summer of 1916. So my sophomore year I started Latin. People with German names, like ours (Schaaf), were not persecuted or put into concentration camps, but we were not exactly popular.

My father made no secret of his German sympathies and refused to believe the stories of German atrocities. Since my mother was very pro-British, the family arguments were terrible; we had a nice little war at home.

Things became very different after we entered the war. I learned to knit for the Red Cross, using that rough khaki wool that was supplied; mother worked with some organization that rolled bandages. Dad became **very** quiet. At high school, several groups were doing war work. The 1918 annual has pictures of the boys who had enlisted and a long list of younger boys who quit school in the spring to go and work on farms. America had to feed the world. My current "steady" went out to a wheat farm in western Kansas and came home after harvest full of stories about the food, the bunkhouse and his fellow workers.

There were no ration books, but we were urged to save on many foods. There were meatless and wheatless days and the magazines were full of recipes for eggless, butterless and tasteless cakes. Mother made **one** really good fruit-cake without eggs or butter, and using chopped carrots to replace much of the fruit.

Fashions began to change. Army nurses and Salvation Army girls cut their hair short, because it made it easier to keep clean and civilian women began to follow this example. Many girls my age also got "bobs," but my father and many others refused permission. They thought it made a girl look "fast." Skirts began to creep upwards, too, as the war went on — the first step toward the knee-length skirts of the twenties.

There was the Liberty Loan for the war; we began to read about airplanes used in battle; and the casualty lists got longer. Finally the United States was building ships faster than the subs could sink them and the war was over. The false armistice was celebrated and then the real Armistic Day on Nov. 11, 1918. The schools and practically everyone marched in the big parade. I helped carry an enormous flag that almost spanned O Street. I don't know who was left to watch the parade.

Epidemic

The Armistic Day crowds and the excitement seemed to stir up the flu epidemic which had started in Lincoln about Oct. 5 and was thought to be dying out by Nov. 11. More and more cases were reported; schools and churches were closed and people started wearing masks in public.

On Nov. 18 my mother was stricken and my brother Ade the next day. The doctor told them to stay in bed and that he would find us a nurse. He came twice a day but no nurse appeared. Father stayed home to help us manage my brother who was delirious. In two more days, father and our four-year-old sister took to their beds with very high temperatures.

Miss Stahl, a registered nurse who had rented a room with us for 10 years, took herself off a stroke case and came home to 24-hour duty. Mother and my brother were out of danger and the other two patients upstairs were much improved when Miss Stahl was stricken. She was the worst case of all and we almost lost her.

All this time, my next sister, then 13, did not have a sign of the flu. I had a very light case. Dr. F told me to do my best, gave me some tiny red pills to take if needed to keep me on my feet and told me to rest all I could. I stayed downstairs and cooked. The stores delivered what we needed. Irene carried trays and washed dishes.

Who changed the beds? Who did the washing? I haven't the least idea; all the family who might help me remember are gone, and the sister who was 4 then was too young. But we all survived to celebrate a strange Christmas: almost no gifts or decoration and very little activity.

Lincoln had 219 deaths from the flu out of 4,000 reported cases in the 1918 epidemic.

On September 16, 1916, the Nebraska National Guard was sent to the Mexican border prior to their recall in 1917 as war with Germany became imminent. Here the troops march to the Burlington depot for departure.

DOCTORS, ETC.

When I was a child, there was no health care as we know it today. One did not go to a doctor for regular check-ups, you saw him only when you were sick. There were few specialists and the family doctor took care of young and old. Until my children were born in the 1930s, I had never heard of a pediatrician. Very few folks were vaccinated against smallpox unless an epidemic came to town and few children were given shots against other less serious diseases.

If possible, most people stayed at home even when they were so ill that they had to be in bed for several days — or weeks. Most feared and hated hospitals and thought of them as places where people went to die. In 1907, St. Elizabeth's was the only large general hospital in Lincoln. A few doctors owned hospitals of their own, usually in large, former private homes.

You had a serious operation in a hospital (and I remember there were many more appendix removals in those days than today) but your family doctor might take out your tonsils in his office, cutting them off with a wire snare. That was the only time we ever saw him in his office as he still made house calls.

People still stayed home to be sick. For measles and other less dangerous ills, the Health Department tacked up a large yellow sign beside the front door. My father went to stay at a hotel when we were quarantined in yellow. Every morning he came to talk to Mother through the front door and to find out what errands she wanted him to do that day.

When my brother, Ade, had diphtheria in 1909, the sign was red (for danger), and Father also had to be quarantined in with the rest of us. I well remember the evening when we all stood around the dining room table, listening as consultant doctors told us how serious things were with Ade. That night we were all given antitoxin shots. Ade's case was complicated by spinal meningitis and the doctors said he would not live, or that he would have serious brain damage if he did survive. Ade *did* recover, but he lost several months of school and therefore repeated the second grade the next year.

After he was up and around, we spent the night with friends while our house was being fumigated. This is no longer done—now the place is just given a very special cleaning. But in 1909, a crew came and burned sulphur candles all over the tightly closed big house. The house was then aired for a day, with borrowed fans all over the place. We returned the next night to find a horrible blackened mess. The only good thing was that Mother had not yet started spring housecleaning when Ade got sick, as it would have been necessary to do it all over again.

Hospitals would not accept patients who were suffering from diphtheria, smallpox and other serious red card diseases, and so a "pest house" was set up for hotel residents and transients who became ill. Volunteers who had recovered from smallpox rented a house at 609 Hatch Street, two blocks south of South Street. I never saw the place, but I always thought of it as being "way out in the country." The pest house, established in 1901 after a big smallpox epidemic had hit Lincoln, was in use until the late 1920s.

For serious illness at home, the doctor found you a registered nurse (we called them "trained nurses") who would take house jobs. Except during the 1918 flu epidemic, there were usually plenty of nurses available in Lincoln. Small towns and farm homes had fewer nurses nearby, so neighbors and friends often came in to help when serious illness struck a household there.

We had three nurses "around the clock" for Ade, but for most cases, we had one nurse on 24-hour duty (she was paid $3 per day then). We would put up a cot in the sickroom for the nurse to snatch a bit of sleep. Mother would sit by the patient for part of the night while the nurse rested.

She would shade the 25 or 30 watt bulb hanging from the ceiling with a cone of letter paper (that was safe enough with those old fashioned low wattage bulbs). We didn't notice how dim they were because we had been brought up with even dimmer kerosene lamps.

"Trained nurses" were often starchy tyrants who brusquely ordered the family around while taking tender care of the patient. They would do no housework except to carry the patient's trays. One could also hire "practical nurses" who would work for even *less* pay and would also help with the housework. These early years of the twentieth century were not very far removed from the time of Charles Dickens' ignorant, dangerous Sairy Gamps. But our nurses were mostly fine, dedicated women who saved many lives in cases like pneumonia, for which there was no treatment (before antibiotics) except very good nursing.

Before antibiotics were discovered, almost any operation was serious and dangerous. By 1910, anesthetics and antiseptics were in use, so operations were not so horrible as they had been during the Civil War. However, medical knowledge made some progress in each war, and the first World War advanced knowledge and techniques enormously.

Almost all women had their babies at home, with a nurse, a neighbor, or a family member to help. Many a country neighbor had delivered the baby before the doctor had time to arrive.

For older patients, nothing like the modern nursing and convalescent homes had yet been invented. In Lincoln, a few women nursed convalescents in their homes and a few others would take helpless or senile old people. The rich stayed at home and hired a nurse. My mother knew one rich old lady who could never keep any help because she fed them so poorly. Really impoverished people went out to the "Poor Farm," maintained by the county, out northwest of town. (This big house is still there, now a private home). At the county farm able-bodied old men helped with the outside work and active old women helped with the nursing and the housework.

Houses and families were large and most people kept grandpa and grandma at home. Often a maiden aunt would come and help. Many a daughter of a large family would remain unmarried and stay at home to care for aged parents.

My mother had a close friend in David City, who for many years kept her mother-in-law, helpless from a stroke, bedfast in her home. We used to visit in David City almost every summer, staying at the old Perkins Hotel (which has just been demolished after a long and useful life). We always called on Mother's friend, visited the old lady (who was enormously fat) and sometimes the younger Mrs. E. would even ask us to dinner. How did she manage? She also raised her own large family in those years.

People knew very little about nutrition then and less about the causes of strokes and high blood pressure. It was considered normal and even desirable to gain weight as you grew older. I knew of friends who were trying to *gain* weight, but I never heard of anyone trying to *lose*. Nobody ever tried to balance the diet, we just ate what we liked. We all ate too much fat and sugar, perhaps because most houses were so cold.

Things are very different, now that vaccination, sanitation and education have practically wiped out many diseases. Children now are immunized against most things before they go to school. In 1920, ten to twenty percent of the babies died before their first birthdays, and more died in the dangerous "second summer" after they had been weaned. Poor refrigeration and careless handling caused some food to spoil. We were lucky, living in a modern small city and having a very careful mother. Mother had recovered from typhoid fever in 1886 and lived in great fear of this disease all the rest of her life. At the first sign of fever, she would start boiling everything and keeping the patient's dishes separate. About the time of the first World War, when the cause of typhoid was known and a "Typhoid Mary" who carried the germs was discovered working as a food handler in Lincoln, Mother's fear only increased.

About this time there was a campaign against flies, and also one against spitting on sidewalks. There were newspaper ads with frightful pictures, and even some school lessons about the dangers of flies and spitting. There were lots of flies. They clustered black on the window screens and screened door to the kitchen when meals were cooking. Some got into the house, of course, and there were sheets of flypaper on the kitchen counters and hanging in strips from the ceiling. Women would set the table for a meal and then cover it with a thin cotton cloth until it was time to serve. There might be a fly or a wasp in an open jar of jam on the table and you looked carefully before taking a spoonful.

The schools joined the papers in the campaign against spitting. This could carry tuberculosis; a boy in my grade school class died at 13 of what we called "consumption." His was my first funeral and the entire class attended.

Many people thought that unpleasant smells would purify the air and ward off illness, and in school there was likely to be at least one child in each class wearing an asafetida bag around his neck.

Perhaps they were not the "good old days" after all.

House calls

Yes, a doctor made house calls — day or night. At first he used a horse and buggy, but soon he was driving one of the first automobiles. People still called the doctor only when illness was very serious. My mother and many other women became very good at diagnosis and home treatment for many ills.

Mother had bothered her David City doctor so much with her first children that he finally told her, "What did your mother on the farm do for you when you were a child? She couldn't call her doctor every day." So she learned to do for herself much of the time.

She could take temperatures quite well by feeling your forehead and hands. I remember her telling dad, "Frank, go call the doctor. Tell him that Ade has a very high fever." She kept a special "clean" rag-bag, full of soft white pieces, washed and ironed and ready for bandages. She made mustard plasters and hot onion poultices. We were glad that she seldom gave any of us a laxative, as hers was castor oil. We were usually healthy, so she must have been doing something right. However, she had an unreasoning fear of vaccination, as did most people at that time, and she never had any of us done. When I was in high school (in 1918) a boy was found in school, already broken out with smallpox. Panic resulted and for more than a week each student who could not show a vaccination scar had to report to the nurse every morning before school. On two mornings I showed a slight temperature and was sent home. There was then no law that a child must be vaccinated, but the school had a perfect right to exclude him with a fever.

Of course, we had all the common childhood diseases, as soon as I went to school and brought everything home to the others. I missed so much school in the first grade, whooping for months in the spring, that mother made me repeat the first grade the next year in Lincoln.

I had bronchitis at least once every winter. Mother rubbed my chest with goose-grease and turpentine, and set up a steam kettle and a tent for the bad nights. She had a little alcohol burner to keep the water boiling.

Irene was subject to quinsy, which the dictionary calls "superating tonsilitis." The doctor came several times to lance her tonsils and finally removed them one summer. Therefore, all we others went to his office to have ours out, too.

None of us ever had mastoid trouble, but this was a common and much feared affliction before antibiotics. One child might have an earache, which Mother treated with a few drops of warm oil in the ear. Often a child would come to school with a flannel cloth around his head — for his earache.

Country doctors managed the best they could, with few small town hospitals and many farm patients. They often had to do an emergency operation on a kitchen table. We never had any operations, serious or not, but once our doctor had to come out to set Ade's arm after he broke it cranking a friend's Ford. After the doctor put a cast on Ade's arm, he told Mother to take it off after four weeks. I didn't see this done, but heard about it. They gouged out a trough in the cast and kept it full of vinegar until the plaster softened. Then the cast could be cut off.

Doctors did not have to spend so many years in medical school or earn so many college credits before enrolling in medical schools in those days. Our David City doctor spent two years at Rush Medical College in Chicago after two years at a small college. In the latter part of the nineteenth century, many young men learned medicine by working for some years with a practicing physician, a sort of apprenticeship, which was called a preceptorship. There were a lot of small, second-rate "medical" schools then, which turned out second-rate doctors. Until the first decade of the twentieth century, when examinations and certificates began to be given by the state, a man could go out, call himself a doctor, and practice.

Our doctor was a good family friend who came swiftly when called and then seemed to have all the time in the world for us. We trusted him completely and never questioned any of his judgments. He came, washed his hands, sat down beside the bed, and opened his big black bag. We felt better merely because he was there. He seldom wrote a prescription to be filled at the drug store. Instead, he often left a small bottle of medicine ("one teaspoon in a glass of water") or a few pills which he rolled himself. More often, he measured out some powdered medicine into single doses and folded these into small, thin "medicine papers."

This was the height of the patent medicine period (not really patent). Most newspapers had a whole section of ads for these "medicines" with glowing testimonials from satisfied users. Traveling medicine shows pushed their special brands, using bands or carnival acts to draw crowds. The barkers' message for the gullible was that their brands would cure anything from the itch to cancer, from the common cold to tuberculosis. Most of them were harmless (and useless), but when soothing syrups, containing narcotics were given to babies, that was very dangerous. Most patent medicines were almost entirely alcohol and a nice, sober member of the WCTU could get addicted to them.

Mother dosed us with such home remedies as lemon juice in hot water, and she also used a lot of soda—both externally and internally. For coughs, she used a spoonful from a bottle of rock candy in rye whiskey that she kept on the top shelf of the tall cupboard. This was called Rock and Rye. Once in a while when the doctor was called for a very bad cold, he would leave a bottle of cough syrup, red with a wild cherry flavor. He was a good man, and if he did not have the modern miracle drugs in his black bag, at least he did not bleed his patients to death, as George Washington's doctors did to him.

We did not like our dentist and we were afraid of him. The old slow-speed drill of those days was very painful and few dentists gave shots for pain before starting to work on one of your teeth. Most people simply endured the toothache as long as possible. Or one could buy medicine to drop in the cavity or rub on the gum, but when the pain and the swelling got too bad, they finally had the tooth pulled.

Many people had full sets of dentures by thirty. If a baby tooth went bad, it was pulled before its time and the permanent teeth came in very crooked. There was very little orthodontistry and children were not taught to care for their teeth until the schools began campaigns to use a toothbrush regularly. Before that, one often saw a child with green edges around the gum line.

Most dentists did not have X-ray equipment, nor did they put in many inlays in those days. They usually filled a cavity with gold or silver amalgam. They used crowns more often than today. In the 1920's and 1930's I lost three first molars which had been crowned when I was eighteen. I kept "forgetting" to keep appointments which Mother would make for me, so the cavity got larger and harder to fill and was finally crowned.

My father had unusually good teeth. He never saw a dentist for years. Finally, in 1929, after his whole jaw had ached for weeks, a dentist told father that he had serious gum disease and must have all his teeth pulled at once. Father never went back to the dentist and began to take strong painkillers, then easily available. Probably this helped to cause his automobile accident in August. When he died in October we were told it was from the effects of the accident, which had seemed minor at the time. (Or did the *bad teeth* kill him?)

85

LINCOLN'S OLD AUDITORIUM

The old Municipal Auditorium in Lincoln was dedicated in 1900, with a concert by Paderewski, and was a valuable addition to the city until it burned down in the early morning dark of April 1928. The University of Nebraska Coliseum took over many of the functions for years. But it was 1958 when the city opened Pershing Auditorium at 15th and N streets. That occasion brought this comment in a Lincoln newspaper:

After nearly 29 years, four building bond elections, two State Supreme Court decisions, and a couple of wars, Lincoln again boasts a city auditorium.

Many people objected to the planned site and fought to have the new building at 33rd and O, on the Woods Park tract. Now the new building sits on the site of the old Lincoln High School, a grade school, and the Board of Education building.

Very few of my friends can even remember the old auditorium. It sat facing the Cornhusker Hotel, had a little mini-park to the north, and many trees around it. It had a faintly military air, like an armory. There were two squat towers on the front corners and crenelations around the roof.

The inside seemed very large to a child, and the high roof was supported by a wonderful forest of beams and trusses, all made of wood. The fire must have been a spectacular sight.

There was a balcony, with a slide projector above. Lectures by famous explorers were popular attractions, and I was taken to see several. The slides were hand-painted — there was no color photography then — and the high colors lent an additional air of unreality to these scenes of strange countries.

The lecturer would show us the main features with a long pointer, and then sound a clicker in his hand for a new slide, which was often upside down on the screen. The children in the audience would yell and whistle, and the boys stamped their feet.

My parents were great concertgoers and took us to hear a few popular singers and other artists. I heard Schumann-Heink and Caruso, and Paderewski on one of his return visits.

But I was not there on the night Amelita Galli-Curci's program was interrupted by a shirttail parade of Nebraska football fans. She stood aside as the boys paraded across stage and applauded them. She was not a typical opera singer, but was young, lovely and slim; and that night she showed no artistic temperament. Someone brought her the sheet music of a Nebraska song and after the boys left, she handed this to her accompanist and sang the song before continuing with her program.

I saw Harry Lauder and Will Rogers and many other popular entertainers and spent many happy hours in the old building. When I graduated from the eighth grade in 1915, Lincoln was small enough that all the graduates could sit on bleachers built on the stage. University graduations were held there until the Coliseum was built. And the Military Ball in December was always there, as the building had a very good dance floor.

Military ball

The dresses were ugly in 1925, when I danced at the Military Ball. My dress was made of pretty material, a flame chiffon skirt in many layers and points and a silver lace top. But the skirt ended at my knees and the top went down to my hips. One popular Lincoln girl wore a skirt made of countless layers of fringe. Nineteen twenty-five and 1926 were the top years of the John Held-type boy and girl and the Charleston.

Many churches put on a big bazaar at the auditorium every fall to raise money for the building fund. Few had parish houses with rooms big enough to hold a bazaar, and they often rented the auditorium. Booths were set up around the walls, and gift items from babies' bootees to cookies and other foods were sold.

Many famous cooks contributed their specialties. Mother always bought a jar of salad dressing at one bazaar. This was the old "boiled dressing" (not boiled at all) made with egg yolks and real cream and perfect for potato salad.

There was often a fortuneteller, and I helped out on many occasions because my parlor trick was reading palms. I got so good at this that I was actually paid for the readings in the twenties. (I met my future husband while telling fortunes at a Halloween party in 1925).

One huge and highly successful bazaar was held in 1918, to raise money for the war. Many groups helped with this and people performed concerts and skits on the stage.

After the state basketball tournament was set up, the Class A games were held there. University groups put on shows there and the Kosmet Klub had given a play there the night before the fire.

Many of these entertainments and attractions were little different from those seen today at Pershing and the Bob Devaney Sports Center. We used to see minstrel shows, which now have gone the way of vaudeville. Minstrel groups were very popular then, and we were taken to at least one each winter.

A white man (the interlocutor) sat in the middle at the back, with two rows of men in black makeup. The end men of the front row were the top comedians of the group and carried on a comic dialogue with the interlocutor. Comedians were still telling ethnic jokes and using the old down-putting names like "nigger" and "wop".

The whole troupe burst into song at the slightest excuse. Their singing usually was very good, and their awful jokes sounded fine to our unsophisticated group.

Now each high school fills Pershing Municipal Auditorium for its own graduation ceremony. At these affairs you can still see the family groups like those of my childhood. Concerts are attended by groups of the same age and the same tastes. I don't think my parents would have taken us to hear some of the modern musical groups.

The interior of the old Lincoln City Auditorium at 13th and M Streets looking from the stage.

DADDY'S 'JELLY'

My father must have inherited a gene from some wild Vandal ancestor — he was so unlike his good, saving German parents. His father sold the crops and put the money in the bank. There it stayed until Grandpa bought an expensive piece of equipment or another farm. He paid small bills in silver from a deep purse with a small top opening. His womenfolk paid the grocery bills with butter and eggs. In the eighties and nineties, not much cash was needed. There were the three sons to work the farm and a hired man would help for his keep and very little money.

My father hated the farm and since Grandpa did not pay his boys regular wages, Father never learned to manage well. He used to carry a fat roll of bills in a rubber band, with a big bill on the outside. To pay for small purchases, he would peel off a bill from the roll and put the change in his right trouser pocket, where he liked to jingle the silver coins. That pocket was always wearing out. At night he put his change on the dresser and this was Mother's main source of income. Father thought she could run the house on nothing, as his mother did. But he made wine.

His father drank beer and his mother made wine from the fruits of the countryside — her elderberry wine was famous. Mother, on principle, would not do this and non-cooking Father learned how. I suppose there must have been books on wine-making, even then.

Teetotallers

We didn't know anyone who used wine. Our friends and neighbors were Methodist and Presbyterian prohibitionists. Many of them belonged to the WCTU or the Anti-Saloon League. Lincoln was usually dry under the local option law. When saloons were legal here, they blossomed along downtown O Street. We girls were taught to walk on the opposite side of the street from their doors. Nobody we knew "drank" or served wine with their meals or used it in cooking.

89

Father served his sweet wines with cookies to evening guests, usually men, as most ladies refused to taste the wine. His regular production was made from Welch's grape juice — not really suited for wine. I don't suppose one could buy juice from California wine grapes, as I did a few years ago.

Mother taught our youngest sister to call the wine Daddy's "jelly" so the neighbors would not know of father's activities. Our youngest was very hospitable and liked to treat the other children. One day, not finding any lemonade or pop, she got an open bottle of grape "jelly" from the ice-box. An older boy poured a little wine into each of eight or ten water glasses, not enough to hurt the children. But one of the little boys reported to his mother, "that was the bitiest jelly I ever tasted." The story got back to mother and she was more embarrased than ever.

Small glasses

Father served his wine in very small glasses and got the cookies from the ever-full jar in the kitchen. We children would always be in bed by this time of night and I know the story from Mother. As she grew older and more tolerant, she started to tell us these stories of our earlier life. Marjorie, who was only three or four when she shared the "jelly," does not remember this. But when father made the dandelion wine, in 1916 or 1917, I was old enough to see the whole thing.

Father hired some small boys to pick the dandelions, which were plentiful around us. We children all helped to pull off the yellow heads and put them into the big canning kettle on the back steps. When this was full, father dumped the blossoms into the ten gallon crock in the basement "fruit room," his work room. When he had enough (and it took a lot of flowers), he poured on boiling water, and added sugar and some cut-up lemons. Then he covered the crock with a large wet piece of sheet from mother's "clean" ragbag. When the mixture had cooled enough, he added yeast.

The crock began to work and bubble in the usual way. After a week or so, father added more brown sugar, which mother had to dissolve on the stove upstairs. In fact, she always did most of the work, while he stood by, telling her how to do it. At this time, he found that he must make a trip to Florida, at once. There he was involved in an orange grove operation. As usual with his ventures, he was too far ahead of the Florida boom and lost the whole thing. To invest in Florida, he had sold his second good Butler County farm.

Directions

Before he left, he carefully wrote out the remaining directions for the wine, warning mother not to change one thing. Then he caught the train, to be gone three weeks.

When we were supposed to add more sugar, Mother said, "This recipe must be wrong. Anyway, his wines are always too sweet." So she added only one-half the amount of brown sugar called for. All would have been well, except that she could never learn to keep things to herself. She told Father, while they were straining the mixture after he got home. He was furious and complained for weeks.

He never felt proud of this wine, and when the time came, he sealed it in quart canning jars, instead of bottling and corking it. If a friend complimented on the flavor, Dad would give him a quart to take home.

One night about two years later, he served the dandelion to some friends, Mr. and Mrs. Bennett, who had been playing whist. I was now old enough to stay up and was reading a book in the back parlor, so I heard it all.

The Bennetts had been our neighbors in David City and were much older than my parents. Mother always asked them to holiday dinners and summer picnics, along with some other old people, my music teacher and a few other friends who lived alone.

'Best ever'

Mr. Bennett was a character. I thought he was very old, and he was probably 60. He was a dandy — always wore spats and carried a cane. Years later, when he was 85, he was hit by a car as he was riding his bicycle on O Street. He had lived in New York at one time and was an "authority" on everything. Now he tasted the wine, smelled it, tasted again and said, "Frank, this is the best wine you ever made. It tastes like fine old sherry." He called it "Oporto," which was meaningless to us. But after that we always called the dandelion wine (or what there was left of it) Father's "Oporto."

He never again gave away a quart jar of the precious stuff and served it only to special friends and in the smallest wine glasses in the house. But never in his life would he admit that he really owed it all to Mother and her stingy ways with the brown sugar. And he never made dandelion wine again.

BEFORE BIG RED

On a recent University of Nebraska football home game Saturday, I noticed my neighbor's Omaha son stop, on his way to Memorial Stadium, to see her. He and his family were all dressed in red. They have had season tickets for many years, so I see them often. When we settled on 28th Street in 1908, there was no such sight. There were few automobiles and Omaha people came to the games on the train.

In those old, slow days a block or two where you lived was a little village by itself. Usually, you were like your neighbors and your friends were like you.

There were football fans in Lincoln and in Nebraska, but not where we lived on 28th Street. All the men in that locality were baseball fans. Boys played baseball on the vacant lot across the street, and the big boys were, never seen throwing the old big football in the street.

Telegraph

Our men talked baseball over the back fence and on the front steps. They read the baseball news in the sports pages, and eagerly bought the extras and the special sports editions that came out after the scores had come to Lincoln by telegraph.

In 1901, when a price war between the Rock Island and the North Western got the round-trip ticket to Minneapolis down to $3, nearly 3,000 fans went on six special trains from Lincoln and Omaha to see the football game (won by Minnesota) in Minneapolis. But no one from our blocks was on the trains.

Things changed slowly. Dad and his friends began to notice and talk about football in the fall of 1914. My father, who had became very pro-German after the European War began, started to read about the young Nebraska coach with the good German name of Ewalt "Jumbo" Stiehm. The name was pronounced "steam," and for four years the Cornhuskers became the Stiehm Rollers.

92

"Jumbo" Stiehm had played football at Wisconsin and came as coach to Nebraska in 1911, starting at $2,000 per year. His Nebraska teams seemed to do better year by year and there was a three-year run, 1913 – 14 – 15, without defeat.

By 1915, our friends really got turned on by football. They only wanted the team to win, and win big. Now you heard football by the back fence, and the men all became instant experts on the game. But not one of them saw a game. I don't believe my father ever did. He planned to see one in October 1915, but a business trip canceled this. He died in 1929, long before the Big Red days.

The years 1913 and 1915 were two of the biggest in all Nebraska football history; in each of those years the Stiehm Rollers compiled records of eight wins, no losses and no ties. The 1913 record included a 7 – 0 win over Minnesota, the 1915 team with the great Guy Chamberlin included Notre Dame among its victims (20 – 19). Nebraska's 1914 record wasn't exactly shameful either: Seven wins, no losses, plus a 0 – 0 tie with South Dakota.

Devaney era

The spotless records of the 1913 and 1915 Nebraska teams were not to be equaled until one of coach Bob Devaney's teams completed a perfect regular season of 10 games without loss or tie in 1965 (only to lose to Alabama in the post-season Orange Bowl), and finally Devaney's national championship 1971 team, which outscored every opponent in a 12 – game regular schedule and then walloped Alabama 38 – 6 in the Orange Bowl.

The first perfect season recorded by Nebraska was in 1902, when Coach W.C. Bummy Booth's men won 10 in a row. Minnesota was defeated that year, 6 – 0.

The 1970 Huskers under Devaney won Nebraska's first national championship with a record that was just barely less than perfect. There were 11 victories, no losses and a 21 – 21 tie with Southern California that season.

Two defeats

In four years, Stiehm and his Rollers earned 35 victories and suffered two defeats (both by Minnesota: in 1911 by 21 – 3, in 1912 by 13 – 0); three games ended in ties. Such a record drew attention elsewhere, so 1915 was to be Stiehm's last season at Nebraska. Indiana offered him $4,500 as coach. He said he would stay here for $4,250, but the Nebraska athletic department could not afford to increase his $3,500 salary that much. Fans talked of making up the difference, but this fell through when the university's faculty began to make objections (a full professor then received about $3,000) and Stiehm left for Indiana.

Since football began at Nebraska in 1890, the teams played on the old Nebraska Athletic Field, laid out by engineering students for intramural sports and situated about where the south end of Memorial Stadium is today. It lay east and west, with roofed stands on the north and bleachers on the south and west. With some exceptions, such as Notre Dame visits to Lincoln, crowds in the early years often did not reach the seating capacity of 8,000.

Coal pile

The east end of Nebraska Field was closed by the university coal pile. This was very large because the power plant heated not only the university buildings but also sold some steam to downtown buildings. There were no organized knot-holers then, and indigent students and small boys stood on the coal pile and watched the game over the east fence. When chased off by the university police, they ran around and climbed up the other side.

One feature of the fall season was the shirttail parade downtown on the Friday nights before games. Students then wore the regulation three-piece suit with a white shirt. It was very shocking when the boys shed coat and vest and pulled the shirttail out of their trousers. They also tied knots in the corners of their big white linen handkerchiefs and wore them as caps. We loved this, when Dad took us down to see the parade. The students snaked in and out of the scanty traffic whooping and yelling while the band played. They also invaded the backstage areas of the theaters, dancing across the stage and disrupting the play or concert more than they had bothered the traffic outside.

You could read about the game in the Sunday paper, but not as much as today. In most non-college cities, the football news was concerned only with Eastern teams, Harvard, Yale and other Ivy League schools. Sometimes one of the more easterly of the teams that now make up the Big Ten was mentioned, as were a few independents such as Pittsburgh and Notre Dame. In 1928, Nebraska left the Missouri Valley Conference and joined the Big Six, which later became the Big Eight.

There were no season tickets in the early days. You bought a ticket at the gate, or earlier at Latsch Brothers store downtown. When, after a few years of so-so teams, football was going great for us in the early 1920s, Mr. Latsch had a bright idea. He said to John Selleck, "Why don't we put the tickets for all the games together with a clip. I think we can sell a lot." They did and soon the university was issuing a season block of tickets. Single admission was $2 for a reserved seat and $1 for general admission.

In the 1920s, there was plenty of room in the new Memorial Stadium and in the 1930s, it was easy to write in early and reserve the same block of seats you had last year. Large blocks were bought by banks, business firms, railroads and private groups who attended games together.

In 1922, I saw Nebraska beat Notre Dame, 14 to 6, on the old Nebraska Field. I think it was the last game played on that field. There had been a huge sign across the east fence, asking fans to contribute to the fund for the new stadium. The sign had been taken down for this last game, so the coal pilers could see the action.

I came back to the university in 1925 to take my degree the next June, and I saw our team play several games in the unfinished new stadium. We did not make an unbroken record, but we won from Illinois, where the great Ed Weir completely stopped the famous Red Grange, and on Thanksgiving Day, we beat Notre Dame again, 17 to 0. My mother had asked her nephew, a student at Notre Dame, to visit us over Thanksgiving. He could hardly eat any dinner after the game and his mother wrote from Montana that she wished he had not come.

All-American Weir

Eastern sports writers and the All-American selection boards were beginning to notice Nebraska by this time and Weir was chosen for all major All-American teams.

There were lots more football fans in Lincoln by the mid-1920s and they (and I) knew lots more about the game. In my high school years, 1915 to 1919, Lincoln High School had good teams and claimed several unofficial state championships. The high schools played on Friday afternoons on several fields about town, because the oval was not built until the 1920s. Some LHS games were played at the old baseball field near 21st and M streets, where the Municipal Swimming Pool later was built. But we usually played at the old university field. The practices were held near the school, except one fall, when a traveling show had set up on that field in the summer and left it full of ruts and big holes. Then the practices were moved to near 27th and A streets, a site which once had been a golf course.

I never saw any football in the very early days of brute strength, pile-up "push-pull" tactics. The games I saw had opened up after the forward pass came into the sport (about 1912) and the basic game was much like it is today. But the two-platoon system is very different. Most of the great players I saw played the full 60 minutes of the game, on both offense and defense. There were very few substitutions.

Everything else is completely different: the great crowds, the radio and TV coverage, longer schedules, bowl games and spring practice, for instance. Teams fly to away games, with no need to practice at a stopover.

And BIG RED!

Now I listen to the games, or watch them on TV, wearing my old red sweater, which I made in the 1960s, when Miller & Paine first let employees wear red in the store on game Saturdays.

CANDLES ON CHRISTMAS TREE

In 1950, when I went to work in the Miller & Paine book store, downtown stores stayed open on Thursday evenings all year. In December, most places opened also on Saturday nights. When the shopping centers were built, their stores were open every night and a few shops downtown began to follow suit.

But when we moved to Lincoln in 1907, almost every store stayed open every night in December, often until 10 p.m. It was said of one place, "They don't close until the last customer has gone home." Clerks worked very long hours.

One afternoon, Mother took us down to see Santa Claus, who looked then just the same as he does now. While she listened, we told him what we wanted for Christmas. Just one thing, because we knew that one major present was all we were going to get. We wanted only what we had just seen in the toy department, as there was no TV to whet our appetites for many wonderful toys, shown all fall on the commercials.

In 1906, our last year in David City, we came to Lincoln by train one day in December, leaving there around 9 a.m. and leaving Lincoln about 5 p.m. I don't remember this trip or the Christmas following it, but I still have the big doll that I received that year, when I was 5. She was made in Germany, as no fine dolls were made in America until World War I cut off toy imports from Europe. She is 32 inches tall and in very good shape, after we had her restrung recently and given a wig and new eyes. Of course, I could read when I got her and never really played with dolls after that.

We are always given a few inexpensive things besides the one big gift. Everything lasted longer then, with more sturdy construction and we never felt deprived. No other children got more and many never had but one gift.

We made the presents for Mother and Dad at school, at the cost of a few pennies for materials. Pen wipers were popular in the days before fountain pens. We also made calendars. We painted a picture and pasted the little calendar on at the bottom. Almost every year at least one child presented a lumpy clay pot, painted in some bright color. As soon as I could crochet and embroider, I made something for my mother. A good neighbor helped me and kept the work at her house so it could be a "secret." By the time I got to high school, I was embroidering luncheon sets and dresser scarves. I also crocheted yards of lace for Mother to sew on corset covers and pillow cases which she used as presents. In those days, most little girls had a needle put in their hands at 5 and were given their first lessons in sewing and fancy-work.

Missing the fun?

I well remember the 1907 Christmas, in the house we rented for most of our first year in Lincoln. After we bought the 28th Street house, the Christmases come back very clearly, especially as they were always exactly the same. Our Protestant neighbors took their children to the parties held on Christmas Eve at Grace Methodist and Second Presbyterian churches. After they put the children to bed, Papa and Mama trimmed the tree. In the morning how did they ever keep the children upstairs while they lighted the candles? It must have been a wonderful sight when the kids came down to see it, but I always thought those children missed half the fun.

We had been helping to trim our tree for a week or more. My tall father always put on the top ornaments, the long spiral garlands, tinsel, popcorn and cranberries, and attached the topmost candles in their holders. He always bought the tallest tree he could find and usually had to cut a lot off the bottom to make the tree fit under our very high (10 feet) ceilings. Mother said, "Frank, why did you pay extra for that monster tree and then come home home and cut off a foot?" I imagine even that enormous tree then cost less than $3. I remember paying only a dollar or two when my husband and I decorated trees in the depression years of the 1930s. We children were not allowed to help when Dad finally lighted the candles on Christmas Eve. After supper he brought in a big bucket of water with a dipper. He had a long-handled lighter, similar to those used in churches. We sat there wide-eyed, thinking he would never get them all lighted.

Santa at the door

Right after the tree was ablaze, there was a loud clamour on the front porch and the sound of sleigh-bells. Dad couldn't leave his post at the fire bucket, so Mother went to the door and admitted Santa Claus, who came ho-ho-ing in and passed out the labelled presents under the tree. These were very few by today's standards and wrapped all alike in white tissue paper and tied with ribbons, mostly red. Any child-wrapped gift was stuck all over with big colored seals. We bought a great envelope full of these for 10 cents.

Mother had made the red velveteen suit, designed to expand or contract to fit all sizes of the friends or relatives who played Santa. The suit was trimmed with white rabbit fur and there was a false white beard that tied around the head under the cap. Thin Santas wore a pillow under the suit in front.

Door barred until morning

Finally Santa picked up his big, lumpy bag and went into the back parlour, where before supper we had hung up our stockings at the fireplace there. Mother closed the sliding doors and we were not allowed to go into the back parlor until morning. I don't think our borrowed Santa filled those stockings **then** — he probably ducked-up the back stairs and came down again to act as a guard on the back parlour doors.

After a late snack, (we had been too excited to eat much supper), we sat around, propping our eyes open, until time for church. They took us all, even the little ones, to midnight mass at the old St. Teresa's church, downtown at 13th and M. I don't suppose we got up very early the next morning, but finally we appeared and opened our stockings. These were just our ordinary long ones, usually our best whites, but sometimes an impatient child had brought down a brown or black one.

Orange was a luxury

There was always an orange (then a seasonal luxury) in the toe, a few tiny toys and a lot of "boughten" candy. We always asked for the highly colored ribbon candy (Christmas mix) and candy canes from the store and this was the only time we ever got any. I don't think I ever ate any of mine. I was always full to the brim of fudge, penuche and divinity that I had helped to make.

Then we put on our coats and went visiting around to see the neighbors' toys, unless some other child got to our house first. One boy ate every stuffed date from the plate Mother had just put out on the center table in the front parlour. Mother said, "John, have some cookies, have some fudge, etc." John snatched up a few more dates and said, "My mom never makes these. We've got all that other stuff at home."

Mother had been working on the dinner since very early morning. We ate at 1 o'clock and always had guests. Now Dad had to put all the leaves in the big square table, then put on the "banquet" cloth. My job was to put the silver on and carry in the innumerable small bowls of relishes and jelly. Every hour or so Dad had to help Mother with the big roaster, while she poured off the fat from the goose. Mother saved every drop of this "goose-grease" which she used in cooking and for medicinal purposes as long as it lasted.

By bedtime, we were all exhausted, but still playing with our new toys and games. Not one of these was ever broken then or very soon. There were no batteries to fail — most toys were wind-up or child-propelled — they worked every time and some for many years.

SEEING HALLEY'S COMET

If I should live three more years — to June 1986 (and this seems likely, as my health is very good and I have an enormous interest in life) — I will be one of the very few to see Halley's Comet for the second time. When the comet last visited Earth, in 1910, I was nine years old. I remember the adults discussing the coming event and I read articles about it in the newspapers. Magazines then were usually illustrated with drawings rather than with photographs and I thought the new visitor would look like these drawings — a little moon with a tail. When, at last, the comet was pointed out to me, I was vastly disappointed. It looked just like any bright star.

I had imagined that the comet would shoot across the heavens like the shooting stars we saw on summer evenings and made wishes on. Astronomers knew that this "star" was out of place and had to be the expected comet. The only stars I knew were in the Big Dipper and if the comet had appeared in this constellation, I might have noticed it. Early the same year, another very bright comet had been visible, the Great Coment of 1910, and many people thought that this one was Halley's.

My family went out to see Halley's in late May or early June. On a clear, warm evening we drove out to a farm on East O Street, where one of my father's friends lived. We were still using the horse and buggy and we took along a picnic supper which we ate just before sunset. Then we walked out into the pasture south of the house. This was on rising ground without trees and we had a good view of the sky low in the southwest.

Seen or unseen?

Mother had borrowed a pair of binoculars. We all saw Venus with the naked eye and there was another bright "star" in the same part of the sky. Mother found this one in the field glasses and told us that it had a tail. We all clamored to look. When I looked, I could see nothing but a blur. I turned the various adjustments, as told, but all I ever saw was just more blurs.

100

(I probably needed glasses, but I didn't know this until years later.) I went home and told everyone at school the next day that I had seen the new visitor to our skies.

I had forgotten my second view, on the Fourth of July, until Meda Knapp jogged my memory. She was a childhood neighbor and I had called to ask about her memories of 1910. Many people of my age do not remember a thing about the comet, but Meda said at once, "Oh, Gladys, don't you remember we all saw it on the Fourth? My mother and yours took all the neighborhood children over to the big vacant lot at 29th and L after we shot off all our fireworks. Your mother was still holding the empty burnt-out tube from a roman candle and the kids all giggled and said they could *smell* the comet." Mrs. Eigenbroadt, Meda's mother, was always thinking up such things for the children to do and my mother was usually with her.

I had been practicing with the binoculars and this time I finally got them focused on the comet, and there was a tiny blob of a tail. Then we all went home and my father shot off our skyrockets.

Outlook for 1986

In 1986, we will not get as good a view of Halley's as we did in 1910. In January, it will be visible for a short time, but perhaps not to the naked eye. Then it will go out of sight behind the sun. On its way back to the other end of its long orbit, it can be seen in the early morning sky, just before sunrise in March and April. Soon it will move so far south that it cannot be seen from our latitude. The United States is not now making any plans to send out a space probe to take pictures of the comet as it passes us. Several other countries are doing so, and I hope we will see the pictures in the magazines, as we did those wondeful shots of Jupiter and its moons a short time ago.

I will practice with my binoculars, so perhaps this time I will be able to see something with them.

Edward Halley (rhymes with valley) was a young Oxford astronomer, studying the orbits of comets in 1682. When Halley's appeared that year, he consulted the old records and found that a comet with a similar orbit had visited the earth in 1607, 75 years before. After checking on the records of numerous earlier apperances, he predicted that this one would reappear in 1757, and published his findings. His comet did not come back until 1759, because its orbit had been slightly altered by a pass close to Jupiter. But this was near enough to his prediction that his studies of the orbit were accepted and the comet was given his name. In 1835 it came again, on schedule, and again in 1910. Further studies of the records proved that Halley's (or a comet with a similar orbit) had been reported for more than 2,000 years.

Isaac Newton's theories of gravity and astronomy were a great help to Halley when he was working out his comet's orbit, and later Halley was

101

able to help his friend, Newton, by paying for the printing of his book *Principia Mathematica*.

There were so many wars, plagues and other disasters in the past centuries that there was usually something of the sort going on when Halley's appeared. For instance, this comet was visible only a few months before the defeat of King Harold of England by William of Normandy in 1066, so people got into the habit of considering its appearance as a harbinger of ill-fortune. Ordinary people could see the stars much more clearly than we can now. The air was clear and there were few bright lights at night.

In 1910, hardly anyone was afraid, but when the papers stated that the earth was going to pass through the tail of the comet, a few people got worried and bought "comet pills" which someone was advertising to protect them. We rode through the tail and nothing happened, so they thought the pills worked.

It's too bad that we are to get such a poor view in 1986. Almost everyone now is well enough educated to enjoy the sight without any fears.

For the future

We hope the planned probes will get some good pictures and that we will learn much more about our old friend who only visits us every 76 years.

In 1910 we were told when Halley's would come again. I was unable to imagine that I would still be alive in 1986 (or in 1983, for that matter). In 1910 few people lived past their seventies. Recently I talked to a friend who is 94 years old and who expects to be out looking for Halley's comet the next time around.

SOME OBSERVATIONS ON TODAY'S MANNERS AND THE NEW MORALITY

When I was growing up, in a middle class family, we lived in some comfort, but without any luxury. Our world was restricted to our immediate neighborhood and our friends were made from schoolmates and the children who lived near us.

Mother made friends easily and belonged to three clubs. She entertained a good deal, usually ladies' lunches and dinners for the neighborhood club. She was often invited to parties but it was hard to get Father to go with her. He enjoyed the theater and concerts, but what he called "sitting around" bored him.

He was not as good at cards as Mother was and although she could (and did) inveigle him into becoming a fourth at whist, and later bridge, he didn't want to attend card parties. He didn't like any sort of formal party or formal wear. He didn't want any of us taught the formal sorts of manners, such as the curtsy for little girls and bowing from the waist for boys.

There was a private school in Lincoln and a few dancing clubs, where such manners were taught. But we and our neighbors were not sent to them. Mother did her best to teach us to say, "Yes, Ma'am" and "Yes, Sir" to our elders and the important "Please" and "Thank you" to everyone, but that was about as far as any formal manners training went. We learned our manners as we did our grammar, from Mother's very good example.

My brother, Ade, learned to get to his feet when a lady entered the room, because he saw Father do so. Ade learned the same way, by example, to open doors for ladies and to stand back while they preceded him. Now, even an old lady has to look sharp near a door. Many modern boys not only won't hold a door for her, but they may even rush through ahead of her so rudely that she has to dodge fast to avoid being run down.

Most men will pull out a chair for a lady in a restaurant, but often in recent times, I have seen a well-dressed man sit down at a table and wait for the attendant to seat his wife. Many people now seem to exist in a world of their own, without giving a thought to the comfort or welfare of others around them.

The most important of our manners lessons were to write thank you notes and bread-and-butter letters. Many young people today are very careless about these important notes. Some misguided mothers even write them for their children. But Aunt Mary would prefer to get a three line note from John, even with misspellings, than to receive a long letter from John's mother.

When I could just barely write and certainly did not spell very well, Mother would set up a model note for me to copy.

> *Dear Aunt Grace:*
> *I am enjoying the book, **The Wizard of Oz** very much. Thank you for sending it to me for Christmas.*
> *With love,*
> *Gladys*

The foregoing letter was also my first lesson in using the social lie, as I already owned the *Wizard* and had read it at least twice. It was my favorite book for many years.

I knew the importance of the RSVP used at the end of an invitation before I knew the words which the letters stand for. So many people now simply ignore the RSVP and a hostess doesn't know how many guests to expect.

Not a mourning matter

I do not mourn the passing of the formal bow and the curtsy, but I think it is too bad that so few men now will rise when even a very old or a very distinguished woman comes into a room. It seems to me that this action was a form of natural respect and innate good manners and owed nothing, or very little, to any formal training. It is too often neglected today.

Some table manners taught to children in my day were silly, like the edict to leave a little food on one's plate, "for Miss Manners," we were told. This was still in vogue in the 1920s, when more than one girl was black-balled for membership in a sorority merely because she ate the lettuce cup under her salad at a luncheon.

Mother thought this custom was silly, as I do, and we were allowed to clean our plates at home and she saw to it that not too much food was on each plate. My parents were still close to the pioneer days when food was hard to come by and everyone cleaned up his plate because he was hungry. But she did stress the basic table manners; such as chewing with the mouth closed and not talking with the mouth full.

Fashions in clothing are a form of manners and those of my childhood were entirely too formal. Also they were too slavishly uniform. When the leaders were all wearing "Merry Widow" hats, all the other women thought they had to appear in just such wide-brimmed hats.

Now one may wear a hat of any size and shape, or none at all. When I was growing up, every woman had to hang her skirts to exactly the same number of inches from the ground. It seems to me that I spent half my time, standing on a table and revolving while mother put pins in the skirt we were making, or letting down. Now a woman can wear her skirt at any length she likes, from a mini-skirt to one that reaches the ground. This independence is good, but it can be carried a little too far.

When I see girls walking into a restaurant in very short shorts and bare feet, I call this much too far. Also this costume looks out of place on the streets downtown. We always had to appear in full "street" outfit, including hat and gloves, whenever we went out of our front doors.

We could, however, play croquet or work in the garden in our own backyards, bareheaded and wearing some old cotton dress. None of us ever dreamed of wearing any form of trousers. I believe that Marlene Dietrich made slacks popular in the late 20s. Bare feet, short shorts and bikinis belong on the beach and not downtown.

Revolutionary and visible

Manners are outward and easy to see and they have not really changed very much, but the change in moral standards is most visible and is nothing short of revolutionary. It is also most different from my day because then the most important thing was to cover up any action which deviated from the general standard of morality, a cover-up which is regarded today as hypocrisy.

When the movie system of stardom was at its height a few years later, a star's love affairs were concealed until they became too blatant to ignore. When the general public finally learned about the affair, the star's popularity with her fans was likely to suffer.

In the old days, there were always unmarried girls who became pregnant (though not nearly so many as today) but they had to quit school as soon as the facts were known; and they were not allowed to come back to school, even if they had married the boy.

Not only girls, but teachers were subject to very strict rules. Of course, very few teachers became pregnant — the very idea was unthinkable. But they could not drink, smoke or get married. If they did any of these dreadful things, they had to resign the teaching job.

Every hurried marriage would set the old ladies to counting on their fingers; perhaps after Mrs. Jones announced that her daughter, Helen, had married John Doe somewhere in Iowa about two months before. If the baby arrived a little early the family always announced that the child was premature. Of course, nobody believed any of this, but it was thought necessary to try the cover-up.

A few strong-minded girls refused to marry the baby's father. These girls were sent away and the pregnancy kept secret, if possible. It was not always possible — gossip was much worse in my day than it is now. If Mary spent several months visiting her aunt in Seattle, the old ladies got their heads together to make the worst story of this visit.

One thing has changed completely. No girl kept her baby then, unless she had married the father before the baby's birth. She and her family covered things up, if they could. The baby was usually given in adoption and the girl resumed her normal life, as nearly as she could manage. I am told that girls who keep their babies now even bring them to school with them when they return to the classroom. If these young mothers are able to support the baby, possibly this is all to the good.

Certainly the modern lack of secrecy and cover-up is a good thing. Many girls "got into trouble" in the old days because they were so ignorant. There was no such thing as sex education of any sort. Our mothers told us nothing — there were no classes on the subject in school and there were no books available to us. I found my mother's hidden *Doctor Book* which I used to study when my parents were out for the evening. This enlightened me and my friends a good deal. The information given in this book didn't go very far, but it was correct as far as it went. Mothers only warned us in general terms. "Helen sits out in a car after a date, spooning with that boy. Don't let me hear of you doing this." Riding around in cars was bad; going out for the evening alone with some boy was bad; my mother preferred group activities for me, and, of course, she was quite right. It was however, easier to be a "good" girl in my day. The aura of chaperonage still hung over us and we were expected to be "good." We were held to a very early curfew as long as we lived at home and our parents always knew where we were. We could go with a boy to the early show; we then had a sundae at Piller's Drug Store and went home on the streetcar. If it was still quite early, we could dance in the front parlor while our parents played cards in the dining room. Very few boys had access to a car — there simply wasn't any place to be alone with a boy. I used to wonder sometimes how the girls who "got into trouble" managed this.

The veterans were different

We began to notice the difference with dates when we got into college and began to date the men who had come back from service in France, during World War I. These were *not* boys and they didn't want to play by the old rules. Often they would not call a girl after she had repelled first advances. They told us to grow up and to stop being little girls. This was known as "having a line" and they all had a line or several. Until I met some of this new tribe, I had never been offered any sort of a drink on a date. But even now, with these strange new types, a girl was somewhat protected by custom. She was not really expected to drink and it was very easy for her to say "No."

After three years of college, I got a junior teaching certificate and taught school for three years. In the smaller towns, I found that dating customs were still much like those in Lincoln when I was in high school. There were group parties and square dances to which the teachers could go together without dates, and there was generally a slow, old fashioned way of life. I enjoyed this very much.

When I came back to Lincoln and the University for a year to get my degree, I soon met my future husband and was engaged before the second semester. By this time the whole dating picture had changed. After prohibition went into effect, people seemed to have a compulsion to drink. It was harder to say "No." There were many more cars and much more freedom, however, most young people still tried to cover up what they were doing. Drinking was still kept under cover and a girl still lost her reputation in a hurry if it became known that she was drinking. There were many rumors of wild parties at fraternity houses.

A personal experience

After I was married, I tasted my first drink of hard liquor. Married women could drink if they managed not to get drunk. Our men would buy straight grain alcohol from a bootlegger and we drank it with canned grapefruit juice. *Ugh!!*

In 1931 we were living in Greeley, Nebraska where my husband, Dean, was an instrument man, working for the state highway department under Project Engineer Steve Gilbert. The Gilberts had rented a little house across the street from the big place where Dean and I rented rooms and they had a houseful of very nice new furniture, so everyone called on them.

One day a delegation of church ladies came to call when I was there and they wanted to see the house. After Mrs. Gilbert had shown them around, they wanted to see the second bedroom. She told them, "Oh, we just use that as a storeroom and it is in a mess." But one of the ladies just pushed by her and opened the door to the "storeroom" where Steve and Dean were busy making home brew. The ladies didn't stay very long after that.

In 1915 (or there abouts) I had tasted beer when father brought home a bottle and told us all to try it. I didn't like the taste, and still didn't care for it when we tried out the home brew at a tasting party in the Gilbert kitchen a few weeks later.

For some reason, I had thought that people didn't get drunk on beer, so I was much surprised when my quiet husband and old sober Steve began to get a little noisy. I paid little attention and went on trying to finish my bottle of the home brew. The two other men from the surveying party were on their third bottles and beginning to get a little noisy, too. Finally, Steve stood up and began to recite *The Shooting of Dan McGrew*. He seemed to know a great many verses and went on and on while his wife and I watched with amazement. Finally he came to the last verse. He threw out his chest on the last line and all the buttons flew off his shirt and rattled on the kitchen linoleum like rain. He disappeared and was found much later sitting on the lowest step of the stairway to the basement. These steps went down from the back porch from a trap-door which he had pulled down behind him. We decided it was time to go home. Walking across the street, I hung on to Dean's arm and felt very strange. I had drunk two bottles of beer and a few sips of a third. When I got into bed, it seemed to go down at the head until I got very dizzy.

This had never happened to me after I had the alcohol and grapefruit juice we had been drinking at parties. That mixed drink was so awful that I never had much of it — it was my custom to nurse one highball for the entire evening. I never learned to like home brew, either, and I could make one bottle last forever. I never went home to a rocking bed again.

With the end of prohibition, everyone we knew seemed to lose the frantic compulsion to drink and began to experiment with mixed drinks and cocktails. I didn't like gin or any sort of sweet cocktail, so after a few years of trying everything I settled down with bourbon and water. When scotch began to be the fashionable drink, I tried that, too, but I soon went back to bourbon.

When we went to visit Dean's cousin in Columbia, South Carolina, we found that this quiet little cousin from Elmwood had become a very typical southern woman, even with a little accent and hard drinking habits. Here I found that my bourbon drinking was approved — almost everyone else was drinking the same. Ellen's husband, however, was always trying to get me to drink some "white mule" out of a quart jar. One of his men had made this years before back in the woods and it had been aging in an oak "kag" for more than twenty years. My fear to try this stuff took me down considerably in his estimation.

These Carolina people seemed to drink all the time and never seemed to show it much. One thing I liked was that all the hostesses served dinner on time. Dinner at eight meant at eight o'clock, and any drinkers had to bring unfinished glasses to the table. Some modern hostesses could do well to copy this. Dinners would not be ruined by standing too long and drinkers would enjoy the meal much more if they had taken only one or two drinks before sitting down. One friend of Ellen's told me that her cook would leave her if she had to keep dinner waiting. And they all had cooks.

One lifetime enough

I don't know why young people get into heavy drinking these days. Perhaps it is their general tendency to try anything, and to overdo the trying. Young people seem to have more money to waste now than we did, and they are certainly drinking from a much earlier age. We were really very unsophisticated when I was first married: Most of us had never heard of any drugs and we would have reacted with horror if anyone had offered any to us. Of course, we were much better off. We were "high" on youth and high spirits, and we really didn't need what liquor we drank. Most of us stopped drinking very much as we grew older.

I am sure that I wouldn't like to have to live my youth over again in today's confused society. I never say to myself, as I hear some friends say, "If I could just live over my twenties (or thirties)." I was lucky to get through mine in good shape. And I am especially thankful that I do not have to raise two adolescents today. Of one thing I feel very sure—I would do my best to enforce the rules of my house.

I feel very deeply that young people living at home and supported by their parents should abide by their parents' rules (relaxed a little to fit modern times). A case illustrating this recently came to my notice.

I heard about one mother whose son came home from an eastern college for Easter vacation, bringing with him his roommate. The roommate turned out to be a silent girl who did nothing during the visit except obey the son's constant orders.

He put the girl's bags in his room. The mother took them to the guest room and told the son that he would have to go to a motel unless he wished to obey her house rules in this, her house. There was a big fight—possibly because it may have been the first time that mother had failed to go along with any whim of her son. I think the mother had every right to set the rules in her house.

What's your hurry

Leaving out any question of morals, I think that any girl is unwise to get into one of these live-in arrangements, especially with a young man who is still in college. She is going to be grown up and saddled with duties and responsibilities for a good many years. Now is the time she should be free and not tie herself down. "What is your hurry," I would like to advise her.

I heard about one live-in couple not far from here. The girl is going to college, has a part time job and contributes to the expenses of the couple. She also does all the work around the apartment while her lord and master sits around and tells her how to do it.

Girls really get very little out of these arrangements. If they are deeply in love, they are desolate when the alliance breaks up. The boy does not usually suffer as much emotional damage as does the girl. Women are not made like men and in spite of what one hears about the modern girls, I do not believe that they can be any different fundamentally from their grandmothers. Simple curiosity and peer pressure have forced them into sex before they are really ready for it, and few of them can tell the difference between real love and simple animal sex urge and infatuation.

"What's your hurry?" I would say to many young people. It is not a very good idea to rush into any new experience. Many of the young seem to be hurrying into experiences with sex, liquor and drugs as if there is to be no tomorrow. Perhaps there is none, but irresponsible behavior is not going to make one's fate any easier. Wait until you have grown up a little, perhaps until you are out of college and have seen a little of the world. "What's your hurry?"